NO FEAR
SHAKESPEARE™

NO FEAR SHAKESPEARE

Antony and Cleopatra

As You Like It

The Comedy of Errors

Coriolanus

Hamlet

Henry IV, Parts One and Two

Henry V

Julius Caesar

King Lear

Macbeth

Measure for Measure

The Merchant of Venice

A Midsummer Night's Dream

Much Ado About Nothing

Othello

Richard III

Romeo and Juliet

Sonnets

The Taming of the Shrew

The Tempest

Twelfth Night

The Two Gentlemen of Verona

The Winter's Tale

NO FEAR
SHAKESPEARE™

Macbeth

DELUXE STUDENT EDITION

There's matter in these sighs, these profound heaves. You must translate. 'Tis fit we understand them.

(Hamlet, IV.i.)

Have you ever found yourself looking at a Shakespeare play, then down at the footnotes, then back up at the play, and still not understanding? You know what the individual words mean, but they don't add up. SparkNotes' *No Fear Shakespeare* will help you break through all that. Put the pieces together with our easy-to-read translations. Soon you'll be reading Shakespeare's own words fearlessly—and actually enjoying it.

No Fear Shakespeare puts Shakespeare's language side-by-side with a facing-page translation into modern English— the kind of English people actually speak today. When Shakespeare's words make your head spin, our translation will help you sort out what's happening, who's saying what, and why.

*sparknotes

ISBN 978-1-4114-7967-8

Distributed in Canada by Sterling Publishing Co., Inc.
c/o Canadian Manda Group, 664 Annette Street
Toronto, Ontario M6S 2C8, Canada
Distributed in the United Kingdom by GMC Distribution Services
Castle Place, 166 High Street, Lewes, East Sussex BN7 1XU, England
Distributed in Australia by NewSouth Books
University of New South Wales, Sydney, NSW 2052, Australia

For information about custom editions, special sales, and premium
and corporate purchases, please contact Sterling Special Sales at
800-805-5489 or specialsales@sterlingpublishing.com.

Manufactured in Canada

Lot #:
2 4 6 8 10 9 7 5 3 1
05/20

sterlingpublishing.com
sparknotes.com

Cover design by Elizabeth Mihaltse Lindy
Interior design by Sharon Jacobs

CONTENTS

PART I

LITERATURE GUIDE

PART II

THE PLAY

PART III

STUDY GUIDE

N O T E S

PART I

LITERATURE
GUIDE

NOTES

CHAPTER

1

CONTEXT

THE MOST INFLUENTIAL WRITER in all of English literature, William Shakespeare was born in 1564 to a successful middle-class glove-maker in Stratford-upon-Avon, England. Shakespeare attended grammar school, but his formal education proceeded no further. In 1582 he married an older woman, Anne Hathaway, and had three children with her. Around 1590 he left his family behind and traveled to London to work as an actor and playwright. Public and critical acclaim quickly followed, and Shakespeare eventually became the most popular playwright in England and part-owner of the Globe Theater. His career bridged the reigns of Elizabeth I (ruled 1558–1603) and James I (ruled 1603–1625), and he was a favorite of both monarchs. Indeed, James granted Shakespeare's company the greatest possible compliment by bestowing upon its members the title of King's Men. Wealthy and renowned, Shakespeare retired to Stratford and died in 1616 at the age of fifty-two. At the time of Shakespeare's death, literary luminaries such as Ben Jonson hailed his works as timeless.

Shakespeare's works were collected and printed in various editions in the century following his death, and by the early eighteenth century his reputation as the greatest poet ever to write in English was well established. The unprecedented admiration garnered by his works led to a fierce curiosity about Shakespeare's life, but the dearth of biographical information has left many details of Shakespeare's personal history shrouded in mystery. Some people have concluded from this fact and from Shakespeare's modest education that Shakespeare's plays were actually written by someone else—Francis Bacon and the Earl of Oxford are the two most popular candidates—but the support for this claim is overwhelmingly circumstantial, and the theory is not taken seriously by many scholars.

In the absence of credible evidence to the contrary, Shakespeare must be viewed as the author of the 37 plays and 154 sonnets that bear his name. The legacy of this body of work is immense. A number of Shakespeare's plays seem to have transcended even the category of brilliance, becoming so influential as to affect profoundly the course of Western literature and culture ever after.

Shakespeare's shortest and bloodiest tragedy, *Macbeth* tells the story of a brave Scottish general (Macbeth) who receives a prophecy from a trio of sinister witches that one day he will become king of Scotland. Consumed with ambitious thoughts and spurred to action by his wife, Macbeth murders King Duncan and seizes the throne for himself. He begins his reign racked with guilt and fear and soon becomes a tyrannical ruler, as he is forced to commit more and more murders to protect himself from enmity and suspicion. The bloodbath swiftly propels Macbeth and Lady Macbeth to arrogance, madness, and death.

Macbeth was most likely written in 1606, early in the reign of James I, who had been James VI of Scotland before he succeeded to the English throne in 1603. James was a patron of Shakespeare's acting company, and of all the plays Shakespeare wrote under James's reign, *Macbeth* most clearly reflects the playwright's close relationship with the sovereign. In focusing on Macbeth, a figure from Scottish history, Shakespeare paid homage to his king's Scottish lineage. Additionally, the witches' prophecy that Banquo will found a line of kings is a clear nod to James's family's claim to have descended from the historical Banquo. In a larger sense, the theme of bad versus good kingship, embodied by Macbeth and Duncan, respectively, would have resonated at the royal court, where James was busy developing his English version of the theory of divine right.

Macbeth is not Shakespeare's most complex play, but it is certainly one of his most powerful and emotionally intense. Whereas Shakespeare's other major tragedies, such as *Hamlet* and *Othello*, fastidiously explore the intellectual predicaments faced by their subjects and the fine nuances of their subjects' characters, *Macbeth* tumbles madly from its opening to its conclusion. It is a sharp, jagged sketch of theme and character; as such, it has shocked and fascinated audiences for nearly four hundred years.

2

PLOT OVERVIEW

THE PLAY BEGINS with the brief appearance of a trio of witches and then moves to a military camp, where the Scottish king Duncan hears the news that his generals, Macbeth and Banquo, have defeated two separate invading armies—one from Ireland, led by the rebel Macdonald, and one from Norway. Following their pitched battle with these enemy forces, Macbeth and Banquo encounter the witches as they cross a moor. The witches prophesy that Macbeth will be made thane (a rank of Scottish nobility) of Cawdor and eventually king of Scotland. They also prophesy that Macbeth's companion, Banquo, will beget a line of Scottish kings, although Banquo will never be king himself. The witches vanish, and Macbeth and Banquo treat their prophecies skeptically until some of King Duncan's men come to thank the two generals for their victories in battle and to tell Macbeth that he has indeed been named thane of Cawdor. The previous thane betrayed Scotland by fighting for the Norwegians, and Duncan has condemned him to death. Macbeth is intrigued by the possibility that the remainder of the witches' prophecy—that he will be crowned king—might be true, but he is uncertain what to expect. He visits with King Duncan, and they plan to dine together at Inverness, Macbeth's castle, that night. Macbeth writes ahead to his wife, Lady Macbeth, telling her all that has happened.

Lady Macbeth suffers none of her husband's uncertainty. She desires the kingship for him and wants him to murder Duncan in order to obtain it. When Macbeth arrives at Inverness, she overrides all of her husband's objections and persuades him to kill the king that very night. He and Lady Macbeth plan to get Duncan's two chamberlains drunk so they will black out; the next morning they will blame the murder on the chamberlains, who will be defenseless, as they will remember nothing. While Duncan is asleep, Macbeth stabs him, despite his doubts and a number of supernatural portents, including a vision of a bloody dagger. When Duncan's death is discovered the next morning, Macbeth kills the chamberlains—ostensibly out of rage at their crime—and easily assumes the kingship. Duncan's sons Malcolm and Donalbain flee to England and Ireland, respectively, fearing that whoever killed Duncan desires their demise as well.

Fearful of the witches' prophecy that Banquo's heirs will seize the throne, Macbeth hires a group of murderers to kill Banquo and his son Fleance. They ambush Banquo on his way to a royal feast, but they fail to kill Fleance, who escapes into the night. Macbeth becomes furious: as long as Fleance is alive, he fears that his power remains insecure. At the feast that night, Banquo's ghost visits Macbeth. When he sees the ghost, Macbeth raves fearfully, startling his guests, who include most of the great Scottish nobility. Lady Macbeth tries to neutralize the damage, but Macbeth's kingship incites increasing resistance from his nobles and subjects. Frightened, Macbeth goes to visit the witches in their cavern. There, they show him a sequence of demons and spirits who present him with further prophecies: he must beware of Macduff, a Scottish nobleman who opposed Macbeth's accession to the throne; he is incapable of being harmed by any man born of woman; and he will be safe until Birnam Wood comes to Dunsinane Castle. Macbeth is relieved and feels secure because he knows that all men are born of women and that forests cannot move. When he learns that Macduff has fled to England to join Malcolm, Macbeth orders that Macduff's castle be seized and, most cruelly, that Lady Macduff and her children be murdered.

When news of his family's execution reaches Macduff in England, he is stricken with grief and vows revenge. Prince Malcolm, Duncan's son, has succeeded in raising an army in England, and Macduff joins him as he rides to Scotland to challenge Macbeth's forces. The invasion has the support of the Scottish nobles, who are appalled and frightened by Macbeth's tyrannical and murderous behavior. Lady Macbeth, meanwhile, becomes plagued with fits of sleepwalking in which she bemoans what she believes to be bloodstains on her hands. Before Macbeth's opponents arrive, Macbeth receives news that she has killed herself, causing him to sink into a deep and pessimistic despair. Nevertheless, he awaits the English and fortifies Dunsinane, to which he seems to have withdrawn in order to defend himself, certain that the witches' prophecies guarantee his invincibility. He is struck numb with fear, however, when he learns that the English army is advancing on Dunsinane shielded with boughs cut from Birnam Wood. Birnam Wood is indeed coming to Dunsinane, fulfilling half of the witches' prophecy.

In the battle, Macbeth hews violently, but the English forces gradually overwhelm his army and castle. On the battlefield, Macbeth encounters the vengeful Macduff, who declares that he was not "of woman born" but was instead "untimely ripped" from his mother's womb (what we now call birth by cesarean section). Though he realizes that he is doomed, Macbeth continues to fight until Macduff kills and beheads him. Malcolm, now the king of Scotland, declares his benevolent intentions for the country and invites all to see him crowned at Scone.

NOTES

8

3

IN-DEPTH REVIEW OF CHARACTERS

MACBETH

Macbeth is a Scottish general and the thane of Glamis who is led to wicked thoughts by the prophecies of the three witches, especially after their prophecy that he will be made thane of Cawdor comes true. Macbeth is a brave soldier and a powerful man, but he is not a virtuous one. He is easily tempted into murder to fulfill his ambitions to the throne, and once he commits his first crime and is crowned king of Scotland, he embarks on further atrocities with increasing ease. Ultimately, Macbeth proves himself better suited to the battlefield than to political intrigue because he lacks the skills necessary to rule without being a tyrant. His response to every problem is violence and murder. Unlike Shakespeare's great villains, such as Iago in *Othello* and Richard III in *Richard III*, Macbeth is never comfortable in his role as a criminal. He is unable to bear the psychological consequences of his atrocities.

LADY MACBETH

Macbeth's wife, a deeply ambitious woman who lusts for power and position. Early in the play she seems to be the stronger and more ruthless of the two, as she urges her husband to kill Duncan and seize the crown. After the bloodshed begins, however, Lady Macbeth falls victim to guilt and madness to an even greater degree than her husband. Her conscience affects her to such an extent that she eventually commits suicide. Interestingly, she and Macbeth are presented as being deeply in love, and many of Lady Macbeth's speeches imply that her influence over her husband is primarily sexual. Their joint alienation from the world, occasioned by their partnership in crime, seems to strengthen the attachment that they feel to each another.

THE THREE WITCHES

Three "black and midnight hags" who plot mischief against Macbeth using charms, spells, and prophecies. Their predictions prompt him to murder Duncan, to order the deaths of Banquo and his son, and to blindly believe in his own immortality. The play leaves the witches' true identity unclear—aside from the fact that they are servants of Hecate, we know little about their place in the cosmos. In some ways they resemble the mythological Fates, who impersonally weave the threads of human destiny. They clearly take a perverse delight in using their knowledge of the future to toy with and destroy human beings.

BANQUO

The brave, noble general whose children, according to the witches' prophecy, will inherit the Scottish throne. Like Macbeth, Banquo thinks ambitious thoughts, but he does not translate those thoughts into action. In a sense, Banquo's character stands as a rebuke to Macbeth since he represents the path Macbeth chose not to take: a path in which ambition need not lead to betrayal and murder. Appropriately, then, it is Banquo's ghost—and not Duncan's—that haunts Macbeth. In addition to embodying Macbeth's guilt for killing Banquo, the ghost also reminds Macbeth that he did not emulate Banquo's reaction to the witches' prophecy.

KING DUNCAN

The good king of Scotland whom Macbeth, in his ambition for the crown, murders. Duncan is the model of a virtuous, benevolent, and farsighted ruler. His death symbolizes the destruction of an order in Scotland that can be restored only when Duncan's line, in the person of Malcolm, once more occupies the throne.

MACDUFF

A Scottish nobleman hostile to Macbeth's kingship from the start. He eventually becomes a leader of the crusade to unseat Macbeth. The crusade's mission is to place the rightful king, Malcolm, on the throne, but Macduff also desires vengeance for Macbeth's murder of Macduff's wife and young children.

MALCOLM

The son of Duncan, whose restoration to the throne signals Scotland's return to order following Macbeth's reign of terror. Malcolm becomes a serious challenge to Macbeth with Macduff's aid (and the support of England). Prior to this, he appears weak and uncertain of his own power, as when he and Donalbain flee Scotland after their father's murder.

HECATE

The goddess of witchcraft, who helps the three witches work their mischief on Macbeth.

FLEANCE

Banquo's son, who survives Macbeth's attempt to murder him. At the end of the play, Fleance's whereabouts are unknown. Presumably, he may come to rule Scotland, fulfilling the witches' prophecy that Banquo's sons will sit on the Scottish throne.

LENNOX

A Scottish nobleman.

ROSS

A Scottish nobleman.

LADY MACDUFF

Macduff's wife. The scene in her castle provides our only glimpse of a domestic realm other than that of Macbeth and Lady Macbeth. She and her home serve as contrasts to Lady Macbeth and the hellish world of Inverness.

DONALBAIN

Duncan's son and Malcolm's younger brother.

4

ANALYSIS OF
MAJOR CHARACTERS

MACBETH

Because we first hear of Macbeth in the wounded captain's account of his battlefield valor, our initial impression is of a brave and capable warrior. This perspective is complicated, however, once we see Macbeth interact with the three witches. We realize that his physical courage is joined by a consuming ambition and a tendency to self-doubt—the prediction that he will be king brings him joy, but it also creates inner turmoil. These three attributes—bravery, ambition, and self-doubt—struggle for mastery of Macbeth throughout the play. Shakespeare uses Macbeth to show the terrible effects that ambition and guilt can have on a man who lacks strength of character. We may classify Macbeth as irrevocably evil, but his weak character separates him from Shakespeare's great villains—Iago in *Othello*, Richard III in *Richard III*, Edmund in *King Lear*—who are all strong enough to conquer guilt and self-doubt. Macbeth, great warrior though he is, is ill equipped for the psychic consequences of crime.

Before he kills Duncan, Macbeth is plagued by worry and almost aborts the crime. It takes Lady Macbeth's steely sense of purpose to push him into the deed. After the murder, however, her powerful personality begins to disintegrate, leaving Macbeth increasingly alone. He fluctuates between fits of fevered action, in which he plots a series of murders to secure his throne, and moments of terrible guilt (as when Banquo's ghost appears) and absolute pessimism (after his wife's death, when he seems to succumb to despair). These fluctuations reflect the tragic tension within Macbeth: he is at once too ambitious to allow his conscience to stop him from murdering his way to the top and too conscientious to be happy with himself as a murderer. As things fall apart for him at the end of the play, he seems almost relieved—with the English army at his gates, he can finally return to life as a warrior, and he displays a kind of reckless bravado as his enemies surround him and drag him down. In part, this stems from his fatal confidence in the witches' prophecies, but it also seems to derive from the fact that he has returned to the arena where he has been most successful and where his internal turmoil need not affect him—namely, the battlefield. Unlike many of Shakespeare's other tragic heroes, Macbeth never seems to contemplate suicide: "Why should I play the Roman fool," he asks, "and die / On mine own sword?" (V.x.). Instead, he goes down fighting, bringing the play full circle: it begins with Macbeth winning on the battlefield and ends with him dying in combat.

LADY MACBETH

Lady Macbeth is one of Shakespeare's most famous and frightening female characters. When we first see her, she is already plotting Duncan's murder, and she is stronger, more ruthless, and more ambitious than her husband. She seems fully aware of this and knows that she will have to push Macbeth into committing murder. At one point, she wishes that she were not a woman so that she could do it herself. This theme of the relationship between gender and power is key to Lady Macbeth's character: her husband implies that she is a masculine soul inhabiting a female body, which seems to link masculinity to ambition and violence. Shakespeare, however, seems to use her, and the witches, to undercut Macbeth's idea that "undaunted mettle should compose / Nothing but males" (I.vii.). These crafty women use *female* methods of achieving power—that is, manipulation—to further their supposedly male ambitions. Women, the play implies, can be as ambitious and cruel as men, yet social constraints deny them the means to pursue these ambitions on their own.

Lady Macbeth manipulates her husband with remarkable effectiveness, overriding all his objections; when he hesitates to murder, she repeatedly questions his manhood until he feels that he must commit murder to prove himself. Lady Macbeth's remarkable strength of will persists through the murder of the king—it is she who steadies her husband's nerves immediately after the crime has been perpetrated. Afterward, however, she begins a slow slide into madness—just as ambition affects her more strongly than Macbeth before the crime, so does guilt plague her more strongly afterward. By the close of the play, she has been reduced to sleepwalking through the castle, desperately trying to wash away an invisible bloodstain. Once the sense of guilt comes home to roost, Lady Macbeth's sensitivity becomes a weakness, and she is unable to cope. Significantly, she (apparently) kills herself, signaling her total inability to deal with the legacy of their crimes.

THE THREE WITCHES

Throughout the play, the witches—referred to as the "weird sisters" by many of the characters—lurk like dark thoughts and unconscious temptations to evil. In part, the mischief they cause stems from their supernatural powers, but mainly it is the result of their understanding of the weaknesses of their specific interlocutors—they play upon Macbeth's ambition like puppeteers.

The witches' beards, bizarre potions, and rhymed speech make them seem slightly ridiculous, like caricatures of the supernatural. Shakespeare has them speak in rhyming couplets throughout (their most famous line is probably "Double, double, toil and trouble, / Fire burn and cauldron bubble" in IV.i.), which separates them from the other characters, who mostly speak in blank verse. The witches' words seem almost comical, like malevolent nursery rhymes. Despite the absurdity of their "eye of newt and toe of frog" recipes, however, they are clearly the most dangerous characters in the play, being both tremendously powerful and utterly wicked (IV.i.).

PART II

THE PLAY

5

Macbeth

THE ORIGINAL PLAY
WITH A MODERN TRANSLATION

William Shakespeare

NO FEAR SHAKESPEARE

CHARACTER LIST*

Macbeth

Lady Macbeth

The Three Witches

Banquo

King Duncan

Macduff

Malcolm

Hecate

Fleance

Lennox

Ross

The Murderers

Porter

Lady Macduff

Donalbain

*See page 9 for an in-depth review of the characters.

ACT ONE

Scene 1

Thunder and lightning. Enter three WITCHES

FIRST WITCH
When shall we three meet again?
In thunder, lightning, or in rain?

SECOND WITCH
When the hurly-burly's done,
When the battle's lost and won.

THIRD WITCH
5   That will be ere the set of sun.

FIRST WITCH
Where the place?

SECOND WITCH
Upon the heath.

THIRD WITCH
There to meet with Macbeth.

FIRST WITCH
I come, Graymalkin!

SECOND WITCH
10   Paddock calls.

THIRD WITCH
Anon.

ALL
Fair is foul, and foul is fair
Hover through the fog and filthy air.

Exeunt

ACT ONE

Scene 1

Thunder and lightning. Three WITCHES *enter.*

FIRST WITCH
When should the three of us meet again? Will it be in thunder, lightning, or rain?

SECOND WITCH
We'll meet when the noise of the battle is over, when one side has won and the other side has lost.

THIRD WITCH
That will happen before sunset.

FIRST WITCH
Where should we meet?

SECOND WITCH
Let's do it in the open field.

THIRD WITCH
We'll meet Macbeth there.

The WITCHES *hear the calls of their spirit friends or "familiars," which look like animals—one is a cat and one is a toad.*

FIRST WITCH
(calling to her cat) I'm coming, Graymalkin!

SECOND WITCH
My toad, Paddock, calls me.

THIRD WITCH
(to her spirit) I'll be right there!

ALL
Fair is foul, and foul is fair. Let's fly away through the fog and filthy air.

They exit.

ACT ONE, Scene 2

Alarum within. Enter KING DUNCAN, MALCOLM, DONALBAIN, LENNOX, *with attendants, meeting a bleeding* CAPTAIN

DUNCAN
What bloody man is that? He can report,
As seemeth by his plight, of the revolt
The newest state.

MALCOLM
This is the sergeant
Who like a good and hardy soldier fought
5 'Gainst my captivity. Hail, brave friend!
Say to the king the knowledge of the broil
As thou didst leave it.

CAPTAIN
Doubtful it stood,
As two spent swimmers that do cling together
And choke their art. The merciless Macdonwald—
10 Worthy to be a rebel, for to that
The multiplying villanies of nature
Do swarm upon him—from the Western Isles
Of kerns and gallowglasses is supplied,
And fortune, on his damnèd quarrel smiling,
15 Showed like a rebel's whore. But all's too weak,
For brave Macbeth—well he deserves that name—
Disdaining fortune, with his brandished steel,
Which smoked with bloody execution,
Like valor's minion carved out his passage
20 Till he faced the slave;
Which ne'er shook hands, nor bade farewell to him,
Till he unseamed him from the nave to th' chops,
And fixed his head upon our battlements.

DUNCAN
O valiant cousin! Worthy gentleman!

ACT ONE, Scene 2

Sounds of a trumpet and soldiers fighting offstage. KING
DUNCAN *enters with his sons* MALCOLM *and* DONALBAIN,
LENNOX, *and a number of attendants. They meet a
wounded and bloody* CAPTAIN.

DUNCAN

Who is this bloody man? Judging from his appearance, I bet he can tell us the latest news about the
revolt.

MALCOLM

This is the brave sergeant who fought to keep me from
being captured. Hail, brave friend! Tell the king what
was happening in the battle when you left it.

CAPTAIN

For a while you couldn't tell who would win. The
armies were like two exhausted swimmers clinging to
each other and struggling in the water, unable to
move. The villainous rebel Macdonwald was supported by foot soldiers and horsemen from Ireland
and the Hebrides, and Lady Luck was with him, smiling cruelly at his enemies as if she were his whore. But
Luck and Macdonwald together weren't strong
enough. Brave Macbeth, laughing at Luck, chopped
his way through to Macdonwald, who didn't even
have time to say good-bye or shake hands before Macbeth split him open from his navel to his jawbone and
stuck his head on our castle walls.

DUNCAN

My brave relative! What a worthy man!

CAPTAIN

25   As whence the sun 'gins his reflection
Shipwracking storms and direful thunders break,
So from that spring whence comfort seemed to come
Discomfort swells. Mark, King of Scotland, mark:
No sooner justice had, with valor armed,
30   Compelled these skipping kerns to trust their heels,
But the Norweyan lord, surveying vantage,
With furbished arms and new supplies of men,
Began a fresh assault.

DUNCAN

Dismayed not this our captains, Macbeth and Banquo?

CAPTAIN

35   Yes, as sparrows eagles, or the hare the lion.
If I say sooth, I must report they were
As cannons overcharged with double cracks,
So they doubly redoubled strokes upon the foe.
Except they meant to bathe in reeking wounds,
40   Or memorize another Golgotha,
I cannot tell—
But I am faint, my gashes cry for help.

DUNCAN

So well thy words become thee as thy wounds;
They smack of honor both. Go get him surgeons.

Exit CAPTAIN *with attendants*

Enter ROSS *and* ANGUS

45   Who comes here?

MALCOLM

The worthy thane of Ross.

LENNOX

What a haste looks through his eyes! So should he look
That seems to speak things strange.

CAPTAIN
But in the same way that violent storms always come just as spring appears, our success against Macdonwald created new problems for us. Listen to this, King: as soon as we sent those Irish soldiers running for cover, the Norwegian king saw his chance to attack us with fresh troops and shiny weapons.

DUNCAN
Didn't this frighten our captains, Macbeth and Banquo?

CAPTAIN
The new challenge scared them about as much as sparrows frighten eagles, or rabbits frighten a lion. To tell you the truth, they fought the new enemy with twice as much force as before; they were like cannons loaded with double ammunition. Maybe they wanted to take a bath in their enemies' blood, or make that battlefield as infamous as Golgotha, where Christ was crucified, I don't know. But I feel weak. My wounds must be tended to.

DUNCAN
Your words, like your wounds, bring you honor. Take him to the surgeons.
    The CAPTAIN *exits, helped by attendants.*

ROSS *and* ANGUS *enter.*

Who is this?

MALCOLM
The worthy thane of Ross.

"Thane" is a Scottish title of nobility.

LENNOX
His eyes seem frantic! He looks like someone with a strange tale to tell.

ROSS
                              God save the king.

DUNCAN
    Whence cam'st thou, worthy thane?

ROSS
                              From Fife, great king,
    Where the Norweyan banners flout the sky
50 And fan our people cold.
    Norway himself, with terrible numbers,
    Assisted by that most disloyal traitor,
    The thane of Cawdor, began a dismal conflict,
    Till that Bellona's bridegroom, lapped in proof,
55 Confronted him with self-comparisons,
    Point against point, rebellious arm 'gainst arm,
    Curbing his lavish spirit; and to conclude,
    The victory fell on us.

DUNCAN
                      Great happiness!

ROSS
                              That now
    Sweno, the Norways' king, craves composition.
60 Nor would we deign him burial of his men
    Till he disbursed at Saint Colme's Inch
    Ten thousand dollars to our general use.

DUNCAN
    No more that thane of Cawdor shall deceive
    Our bosom interest: go pronounce his present death,
65 And with his former title greet Macbeth.

ROSS
    I'll see it done.

DUNCAN
    What he hath lost, noble Macbeth hath won.
                                        Exeunt

ROSS

God save the king!

DUNCAN

Where have you come from, worthy thane?

ROSS

Great king, I've come from Fife, where the Norwegian flag flies, mocking our country and frightening our people. Leading an enormous army and assisted by that disloyal traitor, the thane of Cawdor, the king of Norway began a bloody battle. But outfitted in his battle-weathered armor, Macbeth met the Norwegian attacks shot for shot, as if he were the goddess of war's husband. Finally he broke the enemy's spirit, and we were victorious.

DUNCAN

Great happiness!

ROSS

So now Sweno, the Norwegian king, wants a treaty. We told him we wouldn't even let him bury his men until he retreated to Saint Colme's Inch and paid us ten thousand dollars.

DUNCAN

The thane of Cawdor will never again betray me. Go announce that he will be executed, and tell Macbeth that Cawdor's titles will be given to him.

ROSS

I'll get it done right away.

DUNCAN

The thane of Cawdor has lost what the noble Macbeth has won.

They all exit.

ACT ONE, Scene 3

Thunder. Enter the three WITCHES

FIRST WITCH
Where hast thou been, sister?

SECOND WITCH
Killing swine.

THIRD WITCH
Sister, where thou?

FIRST WITCH
A sailor's wife had chestnuts in her lap,
5   And munched, and munched, and munched. "Give me,"
        quoth I.
"Aroint thee, witch!" the rump-fed runnion cries.
Her husband's to Aleppo gone, master o' th' *Tiger*;
But in a sieve I'll thither sail,
And like a rat without a tail,
10 I'll do, I'll do, and I'll do.

SECOND WITCH
I'll give thee a wind.

FIRST WITCH
Thou 'rt kind.

THIRD WITCH
And I another.

FIRST WITCH
I myself have all the other,
15 And the very ports they blow,
All the quarters that they know
I' th' shipman's card.
I'll drain him dry as hay.
Sleep shall neither night nor day
20 Hang upon his penthouse lid.
He shall live a man forbid.
Weary sev'nnights nine times nine
Shall he dwindle, peak and pine.

ACT ONE, Scene 3

Thunder. The three WITCHES *enter.*

FIRST WITCH
> Where have you been, sister?

SECOND WITCH
> Killing pigs.

THIRD WITCH
> And you, sister?

FIRST WITCH
> A sailor's wife had chestnuts in her lap and munched away at them. "Give me one," I said. "Get away from me, witch!" the fat woman cried. Her husband has sailed off to Aleppo as master of a ship called the *Tiger*. I'll sail there in a kitchen strainer, turn myself into a tailless rat, and do things to him—

SECOND WITCH
> I'll give you some wind to sail there.

FIRST WITCH
> How nice of you!

THIRD WITCH
> And I will give you some more.

FIRST WITCH
> I already have control of all the other winds, along with the ports from which they blow and every direction on the sailor's compass in which they can go. I'll drain the life out of him. He won't catch a wink of sleep, either at night or during the day. He will live as a cursed man. For eighty-one weeks he will waste away in agony.

Though his bark cannot be lost,
25   Yet it shall be tempest-tossed.
Look what I have.

SECOND WITCH
Show me, show me.

FIRST WITCH
Here I have a pilot's thumb,
Wrecked as homeward he did come.

Drum within

THIRD WITCH
30   A drum, a drum!
Macbeth doth come.

ALL
(dancing together in a circle) The weird sisters, hand in hand
Posters of the sea and land,
Thus do go about, about,
35   Thrice to thine and thrice to mine
And thrice again, to make up nine.
Peace! The charm's wound up.

Enter MACBETH *and* BANQUO

MACBETH
So foul and fair a day I have not seen.

BANQUO
How far is 't called to Forres?—What are these
40   So withered and so wild in their attire,
That look not like th' inhabitants o' th' Earth,
And yet are on 't?—Live you? Or are you aught
That man may question? You seem to understand me,
By each at once her choppy finger laying
45   Upon her skinny lips. You should be women,
And yet your beards forbid me to interpret
That you are so.

Although I can't make his ship disappear, I can still make his journey miserable. Look what I have here.

SECOND WITCH
Show me, show me.

FIRST WITCH
Here I have the thumb of a pilot who was drowned while trying to return home.

A drum sounds offstage.

THIRD WITCH
A drum, a drum! Macbeth has come.

ALL
(dancing together in a circle) We weird sisters, hand in hand, swift travelers over the sea and land, dance around and around like so. Three times to yours, and three times to mine, and three times again, to add up to nine. Enough! The charm is ready.

MACBETH *and* BANQUO *enter.*

MACBETH
(to BANQUO*)* I have never seen a day that was so good and bad at the same time.

BANQUO
How far is it supposed to be to Forres? *(he sees the* WITCHES*)* What are these creatures? They're so with-ered-looking and crazily dressed. They don't look like they belong on this planet, but I see them standing here on Earth. *(to the* WITCHES*)* Are you alive? Can you answer questions? You seem to understand me, because each of you has put a gruesome finger to her skinny lips. You look like women, but your beards keep me from believing that you really are.

MACBETH
Speak, if you can: what are you?

FIRST WITCH
All hail, Macbeth! Hail to thee, thane of Glamis!

SECOND WITCH
50   All hail, Macbeth! Hail to thee, thane of Cawdor!

THIRD WITCH
All hail, Macbeth, that shalt be king hereafter!

BANQUO
Good sir, why do you start and seem to fear
Things that do sound so fair? *(to the* WITCHES*)* I' th' name of
        truth,
Are ye fantastical, or that indeed
55   Which outwardly ye show? My noble partner
You greet with present grace and great prediction
Of noble having and of royal hope,
That he seems rapt withal. To me you speak not.
If you can look into the seeds of time
60   And say which grain will grow and which will not,
Speak, then, to me, who neither beg nor fear
Your favors nor your hate.

FIRST WITCH
Hail!

SECOND WITCH
Hail!

THIRD WITCH
65   Hail!

FIRST WITCH
Lesser than Macbeth and greater.

SECOND WITCH
Not so happy, yet much happier.

THIRD WITCH
Thou shalt get kings, though thou be none.
So all hail, Macbeth and Banquo!

FIRST WITCH
70   Banquo and Macbeth, all hail!

MACBETH
>Speak, if you can. What kind of creatures are you?

FIRST WITCH
>All hail, Macbeth! Hail to you, thane of Glamis!

SECOND WITCH
>All hail, Macbeth! Hail to you, thane of Cawdor!

THIRD WITCH
>All hail, Macbeth, the future king!

BANQUO
>My dear Macbeth, why do you look so startled and afraid of these nice things they're saying? *(to the* WITCHES*)* Tell me honestly, are you illusions, or are you really what you seem to be? You've greeted my noble friend with honors and talk of a future so glorious that you've made him speechless. But you don't say anything to me. If you can see the future and say how things will turn out, tell me. I don't want your favors and I'm not afraid of your hatred.

FIRST WITCH
>Hail!

SECOND WITCH
>Hail!

THIRD WITCH
>Hail!

FIRST WITCH
>You are lesser than Macbeth but also greater.

SECOND WITCH
>You are not as happy as Macbeth, yet much happier.

THIRD WITCH
>Your descendants will be kings, even though you will not be one. So all hail, Macbeth and Banquo!

FIRST WITCH
>Banquo and Macbeth, all hail!

MACBETH
Stay, you imperfect speakers, tell me more.
By Sinel's death I know I am thane of Glamis.
But how of Cawdor? The thane of Cawdor lives,
A prosperous gentleman, and to be king
75 Stands not within the prospect of belief,
No more than to be Cawdor. Say from whence
You owe this strange intelligence, or why
Upon this blasted heath you stop our way
With such prophetic greeting. Speak, I charge you.
                                    WITCHES *vanish*

BANQUO
80 The earth hath bubbles, as the water has,
And these are of them. Whither are they vanished?

MACBETH
Into the air, and what seemed corporal
Melted, as breath into the wind. Would they had stayed.

BANQUO
Were such things here as we do speak about?
85 Or have we eaten on the insane root
That takes the reason prisoner?

MACBETH
Your children shall be kings.

BANQUO
                                    You shall be king.

MACBETH
And thane of Cawdor too: went it not so?

BANQUO
90 To the selfsame tune and words. Who's here?

Enter ROSS *and* ANGUS

MACBETH

Wait! You only told me part of what I want to know. Stay and tell me more. I already know I am the thane of Glamis because I inherited the position when my father, Sinel, died. But how can you call me the thane of Cawdor? The thane of Cawdor is alive, and he's a rich and powerful man. And for me to be the king is completely impossible, just as it's impossible for me to be thane of Cawdor. Tell me where you learned these strange things, and why you stop us at this desolate place with this prophetic greeting? Speak, I command you.

The WITCHES *vanish.*

BANQUO

The earth has bubbles, just like the water, and these creatures must have come from a bubble in the earth. Where did they disappear to?

MACBETH

Into thin air. Their bodies melted like breath in the wind. I wish they had stayed!

BANQUO

Were these things we're talking about really here? Or are we both on drugs?

MACBETH

Your children will be kings.

BANQUO

You will be the king.

MACBETH

And thane of Cawdor too. Isn't that what they said?

BANQUO

That's exactly what they said. Who's this?

ROSS *and* ANGUS *enter.*

ACT ONE

ROSS
The king hath happily received, Macbeth,
The news of thy success, and when he reads
Thy personal venture in the rebels' fight,
His wonders and his praises do contend
95   Which should be thine or his. Silenced with that,
In viewing o'er the rest o' the selfsame day,
He finds thee in the stout Norweyan ranks,
Nothing afeard of what thyself didst make,
Strange images of death. As thick as tale
100   Can post with post, and every one did bear
Thy praises in his kingdom's great defense,
And poured them down before him.

ANGUS
                                         We are sent
To give thee from our royal master thanks,
Only to herald thee into his sight,
105   Not pay thee.

ROSS
And, for an earnest of a greater honor,
He bade me, from him, call thee thane of Cawdor:
In which addition, hail, most worthy thane,
For it is thine.

BANQUO
                    What, can the devil speak true?

MACBETH
110   The thane of Cawdor lives. Why do you dress me
In borrowed robes?

ANGUS
                         Who was the thane lives yet,
But under heavy judgment bears that life
Which he deserves to lose. Whether he was combined
With those of Norway, or did line the rebel
115   With hidden help and vantage, or that with both
He labored in his country's wrack, I know not;
But treasons capital, confessed and proved,
Have overthrown him.

ROSS

The king was happy to hear of your success, Macbeth. Whenever he hears the story of your exploits in the fight against the rebels, he becomes so amazed it makes him speechless. He was also shocked to learn that on the same day you fought the rebels you also fought against the army of Norway, and that you weren't the least bit afraid of death, even as you killed everyone around you. Messenger after messenger delivered news of your bravery to the king with praise for how you defended his country.

ANGUS

The king sent us to give you his thanks and to bring you to him. Your real reward won't come from us.

ROSS

And to give you a taste of what's in store for you, he told me to call you the thane of Cawdor. So hail, thane of Cawdor! That title belongs to you now.

BANQUO

(shocked) Can the devil tell the truth?

MACBETH

The thane of Cawdor is still alive. Why are you putting his clothes on me?

ANGUS

The man who was the thane of Cawdor is still alive, but he's been sentenced to death, and he deserves to die. I don't know whether he fought on Norway's side, or if he secretly aided the rebels, or if he fought with both of our enemies. But his treason, which has been proven, and to which he's confessed, means he's finished.

MACBETH
(aside)   Glamis, and thane of Cawdor!
The greatest is behind. *(to* ROSS *and* ANGUS) Thanks for
        your pains.
120 *(aside to* BANQUO) Do you not hope your children shall be
        kings,
When those that gave the thane of Cawdor to me
Promised no less to them?

BANQUO
                              That, trusted home,
Might yet enkindle you unto the crown,
Besides the thane of Cawdor. But 'tis strange.
125 And oftentimes, to win us to our harm,
The instruments of darkness tell us truths,
Win us with honest trifles, to betray 's
In deepest consequence.
(to ROSS *and* ANGUS) Cousins, a word, I pray you.

BANQUO, ROSS, *and* ANGUS *move to one side*

MACBETH
(aside)   Two truths are told,
130 As happy prologues to the swelling act
Of the imperial theme. *(to* ROSS *and* ANGUS) I thank you,
        gentlemen.
(aside) This supernatural soliciting
Cannot be ill, cannot be good. If ill,
Why hath it given me earnest of success,
135 Commencing in a truth? I am thane of Cawdor.
If good, why do I yield to that suggestion
Whose horrid image doth unfix my hair
And make my seated heart knock at my ribs,
Against the use of nature? Present fears
140 Are less than horrible imaginings.

MACBETH

(*to himself*) It's just like they said—now I'm the thane of Glamis and the thane of Cawdor. And the best part of what they predicted is still to come. (*to* ROSS *and* ANGUS) Thank you for the news. (*speaking so that only* BANQUO *can hear*) Aren't you beginning to hope your children will be kings? After all, the witches who said I was thane of Cawdor promised them nothing less.

BANQUO

If you trust what they say, you might be on your way to becoming king, as well as thane of Cawdor. But this whole thing is strange. The agents of evil often tell us part of the truth in order to lead us to our destruction. They earn our trust by telling us the truth about little things, but then they betray us when it will damage us the most. (*to* ROSS *and* ANGUS) Gentlemen, I'd like to have a word with you, please.

ROSS, ANGUS, *and* BANQUO *move to one side.*

MACBETH

(*to himself*) So far the witches have told me two things that came true, so it seems like this will culminate in my becoming king. (*to* ROSS *and* ANGUS) Thank you, gentlemen. (*to himself*) This supernatural temptation doesn't seem like it can be a bad thing, but it can't be good either. If it's a bad thing, why was I promised a promotion that turned out to be true? Now I'm the thane of Cawdor, just like they said I would be. But if this is a good thing, why do I find myself thinking about murdering King Duncan, a thought so horrifying that it makes my hair stand on end and my heart pound inside my chest? The dangers that actually threaten me here and now frighten me less than the horrible things I'm imagining.

ACT ONE

My thought, whose murder yet is but fantastical,
Shakes so my single state of man
That function is smothered in surmise,
And nothing is but what is not.

BANQUO
Look how our partner's rapt.

145 **MACBETH**
(aside) If chance will have me king, why, chance may
          crown me
Without my stir.

BANQUO
                    New honors come upon him,
Like our strange garments, cleave not to their mold
But with the aid of use.

MACBETH
(aside)   Come what come may,
Time and the hour runs through the roughest day.

150 **BANQUO**
Worthy Macbeth, we stay upon your leisure.

MACBETH
Give me your favor. My dull brain was wrought
With things forgotten. Kind gentlemen, your pains
Are registered where every day I turn
The leaf to read them. Let us toward the king.

155 *(aside to* BANQUO*)* Think upon what hath chanced, and, at
          more time,
The interim having weighed it, let us speak
Our free hearts each to other.

BANQUO
Very gladly.

MACBETH
Till then, enough. *(to* ROSS *and* ANGUS*)* Come, friends.

160   *Exeunt*

Even though it's just a fantasy so far, the mere thought of committing murder shakes me up so much that I hardly know who I am anymore. My ability to act is stifled by my thoughts and speculations, and the only things that matter to me are things that don't really exist.

BANQUO

Look at Macbeth—he's in a daze.

MACBETH

(to himself) If fate wants me to be king, perhaps fate will just make it happen and I won't have to do anything.

BANQUO

(to ROSS and ANGUS) Macbeth is not used to his new titles. They're like new clothes: they don't fit until you break them in over time.

MACBETH

(to himself) One way or another, what's going to happen is going to happen.

BANQUO

Good Macbeth, we're ready when you are.

MACBETH

I beg your pardon; I was distracted. Kind gentlemen, I won't forget the trouble you've taken for me whenever I think of this day. Let's go to the king. *(speaking so that only BANQUO can hear)* Think about what happened today, and when we've both had time to consider things, let's talk.

BANQUO

Absolutely.

MACBETH

Until then, we've said enough. *(to ROSS and ANGUS)* Let's go, my friends.

They all exit.

ACT ONE, Scene 4

Flourish. Enter KING DUNCAN, LENNOX, MALCOLM, DONALBAIN, *and attendants*

DUNCAN
Is execution done on Cawdor? Are not
Those in commission yet returned?

MALCOLM
My liege,
They are not yet come back. But I have spoke
With one that saw him die, who did report
5 That very frankly he confessed his treasons,
Implored your highness' pardon, and set forth
A deep repentance. Nothing in his life
Became him like the leaving it. He died
As one that had been studied in his death
10 To throw away the dearest thing he owed
As 'twere a careless trifle.

DUNCAN
There's no art
To find the mind's construction in the face.
He was a gentleman on whom I built
An absolute trust.

Enter MACBETH, BANQUO, ROSS, *and* ANGUS

15 *(to* MACBETH*)* O worthiest cousin,
The sin of my ingratitude even now
Was heavy on me. Thou art so far before
That swiftest wing of recompense is slow
To overtake thee. Would thou hadst less deserved,
20 That the proportion both of thanks and payment
Might have been mine! Only I have left to say,
More is thy due than more than all can pay.

ACT ONE, Scene 4

A trumpet fanfare sounds. KING DUNCAN, LENNOX, MALCOLM, DONALBAIN, *and their attendants enter.*

DUNCAN

Has the former thane of Cawdor been executed yet? Haven't the people in charge of that come back?

MALCOLM

My king, they haven't come back yet. But I spoke with someone who saw Cawdor die, and he said that Cawdor openly confessed his treasons, begged your highness's forgiveness, and repented deeply. He never did anything in his whole life that looked as good as the way he died. He died like someone who had practiced how to toss away his most cherished possession as if it were a worthless piece of garbage.

DUNCAN

There's no way to read a man's mind by looking at his face. I trusted Cawdor completely.

MACBETH, BANQUO, ROSS, *and* ANGUS *enter.*

(to MACBETH*)* My worthiest kinsman! Just this moment I was feeling guilty for not having thanked you enough. You have done so much for me so fast that it has been impossible to reward you properly. If you deserved less, then perhaps my payment would have matched your deeds! All I can say is that I owe you more than I can ever repay.

MACBETH
The service and the loyalty I owe
In doing it pays itself. Your highness' part
25 Is to receive our duties, and our duties
Are to your throne and state children and servants,
Which do but what they should, by doing everything
Safe toward your love and honor.

DUNCAN
                                        Welcome hither.
I have begun to plant thee, and will labor
30 To make thee full of growing. *(to* BANQUO*)* Noble Banquo,
That hast no less deserved, nor must be known
No less to have done so, let me infold thee
And hold thee to my heart.

BANQUO
                                        There, if I grow,
The harvest is your own.

DUNCAN
                            My plenteous joys,
35 Wanton in fullness, seek to hide themselves
In drops of sorrow. Sons, kinsmen, thanes,
And you whose places are the nearest, know
We will establish our estate upon
Our eldest, Malcolm, whom we name hereafter
40 The prince of Cumberland; which honor must
Not unaccompanied invest him only,
But signs of nobleness, like stars, shall shine
On all deservers. *(to* MACBETH*)* From hence to Inverness,
And bind us further to you.

MACBETH
45 The rest is labor which is not used for you:
I'll be myself the harbinger and make joyful
The hearing of my wife with your approach.
So humbly take my leave.

DUNCAN
My worthy Cawdor!

MACBETH

> The opportunity to serve you is its own reward. Your only duty, your highness, is to accept what we owe you. Our duty to you and your state is like the duty of children to their father or servants to their master. By doing everything we can to protect you, we're only doing what we should.

DUNCAN

> You are welcome here. By making you thane of Cawdor, I have planted the seeds of a great career for you, and I will make sure they grow. *(to* BANQUO*)* Noble Banquo, you deserve no less than Macbeth, and everyone should know it. Let me bring you close to me and give you the benefit of my love and good will.

BANQUO

> Then if I accomplish anything great, it will be a credit to you.

DUNCAN

> My joy is so overwhelming it brings tears to my eyes. My sons, relatives, lords, and all those closest to me, I want you to witness that I will bestow my kingdom on my eldest son, Malcolm. Today I name him the prince of Cumberland. But Malcolm isn't going to be alone in receiving honors—titles of nobility will shine like stars on all of you who deserve them. *(to* MACBETH*)* And now, let's go to your castle at Inverness, where I will become even more obliged to you because of your hospitality.

MACBETH

> I'm not happy unless I can be working for you. I will go ahead and bring my wife the good news that you are coming. With that, I'll be off.

DUNCAN

> My worthy Cawdor!

ACT ONE

MACBETH

50   *(aside)* The prince of Cumberland! That is a step
On which I must fall down, or else o'erleap,
For in my way it lies. Stars, hide your fires;
Let not light see my black and deep desires.
The eye wink at the hand, yet let that be
55   Which the eye fears, when it is done, to see.

Exit

DUNCAN

True, worthy Banquo. He is full so valiant,
And in his commendations I am fed;
It is a banquet to me.—Let's after him,
Whose care is gone before to bid us welcome:
60   It is a peerless kinsman.

Flourish. Exeunt

MACBETH

(to himself) Malcolm is now the prince of Cumberland! To become king myself, I'm either going to have to step over him or give up, because he's in my way. Stars, hide your light so no one can see the terrible desires within me. I won't let my eye look at what my hand is doing, but in the end I'm still going to do that thing I'd be horrified to see.

MACBETH exits.

DUNCAN

(to BANQUO, in the middle of a conversation we haven't heard) You're right, Banquo. Macbeth is every bit as valiant as you say, and I am satisfied with these praises of him. Let's follow after him, now that he has gone ahead to prepare our welcome. He is a man without equal.

Trumpet fanfare. They exit.

ACT ONE, Scene 5

Enter LADY MACBETH, *alone, with a letter*

LADY MACBETH
(reading) "They met me in the day of success, and I have
learned by the perfectest report they have more in
them than mortal knowledge. When I burned in
desire to question them further, they made them-
5   selves air, into which they vanished. Whiles I stood
rapt in the wonder of it came missives from the king,
who all-hailed me 'Thane of Cawdor,' by which title,
before, these weird sisters saluted me, and referred me
to the coming on of time with 'Hail, king that shalt be!'
10   This have I thought good to deliver thee, my dearest
partner of greatness, that thou might'st not lose the
dues of rejoicing, by being ignorant of what greatness
is promised thee. Lay it to thy heart, and farewell."

Glamis thou art, and Cawdor; and shalt be
15   What thou art promised. Yet do I fear thy nature;
It is too full o' th' milk of human kindness
To catch the nearest way: thou wouldst be great,
Art not without ambition, but without
The illness should attend it. What thou wouldst highly,
20   That wouldst thou holily; wouldst not play false,
And yet wouldst wrongly win. Thou'ld'st have, great Glamis,
That which cries, "Thus thou must do," if thou have it,
And that which rather thou dost fear to do,
Than wishest should be undone. Hie thee hither,
25   That I may pour my spirits in thine ear
And chastise with the valor of my tongue
All that impedes thee from the golden round,
Which fate and metaphysical aid doth seem
To have thee crowned withal.

Enter SERVANT

ACT ONE, Scene 5

LADY MACBETH *enters, reading a letter.*

LADY MACBETH

"The witches met me on the day of my victory in battle, and I have since learned that they have supernatural knowledge. When I tried desperately to question them further, they vanished into thin air. While I stood spellbound, messengers from the king arrived and greeted me as the thane of Cawdor, which is precisely how the weird sisters had saluted me before calling me 'the future king!' I thought I should tell you this news, my dearest partner in greatness, so that you could rejoice along with me about the greatness that is promised to us. Keep it secret, and farewell."

(she looks up from the letter) You are thane of Glamis and Cawdor, and you're going to be king, just like you were promised. But I worry about whether or not you have what it takes to seize the crown. You are too full of the milk of human kindness to strike aggressively at your first opportunity. You want to be powerful, and you don't lack ambition, but you don't have the mean streak that these things call for. The things you want to do, you want to do like a good man. You don't want to cheat, yet you want what doesn't belong to you. There's something you want, but you're afraid to do what you need to do to get it. You want it to be done for you. Hurry home so I can persuade you and talk you out of whatever's keeping you from going after the crown. After all, fate and witchcraft both seem to want you to be king.

A SERVANT *enters.*

What is your tidings?

SERVANT
The king comes here tonight.

LADY MACBETH
30   Thou 'rt mad to say it.
Is not thy master with him, who, were 't so,
Would have informed for preparation?

SERVANT
So please you, it is true: our thane is coming.
One of my fellows had the speed of him,
35   Who, almost dead for breath, had scarcely more
Than would make up his message.

LADY MACBETH
Give him tending.
He brings great news.

Exit **SERVANT**

The raven himself is hoarse
40   That croaks the fatal entrance of Duncan
Under my battlements. Come, you spirits
That tend on mortal thoughts, unsex me here,
And fill me from the crown to the toe top-full
Of direst cruelty. Make thick my blood.
45   Stop up the access and passage to remorse,
That no compunctious visitings of nature
Shake my fell purpose, nor keep peace between
The effect and it! Come to my woman's breasts,
And take my milk for gall, you murd'ring ministers,
50   Wherever in your sightless substances
You wait on nature's mischief. Come, thick night,
And pall thee in the dunnest smoke of hell,
That my keen knife see not the wound it makes,
Nor heaven peep through the blanket of the dark
To cry "Hold, hold!"

What news do you bring?

SERVANT
The king is coming here tonight.

LADY MACBETH
You must be crazy to say that! Isn't Macbeth with the king, and wouldn't Macbeth have told me in advance so I could prepare, if the king were really coming?

SERVANT
I'm sorry, but it's the truth. Macbeth is coming. He sent a messenger ahead of him who arrived here so out of breath that he could barely speak his message.

LADY MACBETH
Take good care of him. He brings great news.

The **SERVANT** *exits.*

So the messenger is short of breath, like a hoarse raven, as he announces Duncan's entrance into my fortress, where he will die. Come, you spirits that assist murderous thoughts, make me less like a woman and more like a man, and fill me from head to toe with deadly cruelty! Thicken my blood and clog up my veins so I won't feel remorse, so that no human compassion can stop my evil plan or prevent me from accomplishing it! Come to my female breasts and turn my mother's milk into poisonous acid, you murdering demons, wherever you hide, invisible and waiting to do evil! Come, thick night, and cover the world in the darkest smoke of hell, so that my sharp knife can't see the wound it cuts open, and so heaven can't peep through the darkness and cry, "No! Stop!"

Enter MACBETH

55

Great Glamis, worthy Cawdor,
Greater than both, by the all-hail hereafter,
Thy letters have transported me beyond
This ignorant present, and I feel now
The future in the instant.

MACBETH

60   My dearest love,
Duncan comes here tonight.

LADY MACBETH

                             And when goes hence?

MACBETH

Tomorrow, as he purposes.

LADY MACBETH

                        O, never
Shall sun that morrow see!
Your face, my thane, is as a book where men
65   May read strange matters. To beguile the time,
Look like the time. Bear welcome in your eye,
Your hand, your tongue. Look like th' innocent flower,
But be the serpent under 't. He that's coming
Must be provided for; and you shall put
70   This night's great business into my dispatch,
Which shall to all our nights and days to come
Give solely sovereign sway and masterdom.

MACBETH

We will speak further.

LADY MACBETH

Only look up clear.
75   To alter favor ever is to fear.
Leave all the rest to me.

                                      Exeunt

MACBETH *enters.*

Great thane of Glamis! Worthy thane of Cawdor! You'll soon be greater than both those titles, once you become king! Your letter has transported me from the present moment, when who knows what will happen, and has made me feel like the future is already here.

MACBETH

My dearest love, Duncan is coming here tonight.

LADY MACBETH

And when is he leaving?

MACBETH

He plans to leave tomorrow.

LADY MACBETH

That day will never come. Your face betrays strange feelings, my lord, and people will be able to read it like a book. In order to deceive them, you must appear the way they expect you to look. Greet the king with a welcoming expression in your eyes, your hands, and your words. You should look like an innocent flower, but be like the snake that hides underneath the flower. The king is coming, and he's got to be taken care of. Let me handle tonight's preparations, because tonight will change every night and day for the rest of our lives.

MACBETH

We will speak about this further.

LADY MACBETH

You should project a peaceful mood, because if you look troubled, you will arouse suspicion. Leave all the rest to me.

They exit.

ACT ONE, Scene 6

Hautboys and torches. Enter KING DUNCAN, MALCOLM,
DONALBAIN, BANQUO, LENNOX, MACDUFF, ROSS, ANGUS, *and*
attendants

DUNCAN
This castle hath a pleasant seat. The air
Nimbly and sweetly recommends itself
Unto our gentle senses.

BANQUO
          This guest of summer,
The temple-haunting martlet, does approve,
5   By his loved mansionry, that the heaven's breath
Smells wooingly here. No jutty, frieze,
Buttress, nor coign of vantage, but this bird
Hath made his pendant bed and procreant cradle.
Where they most breed and haunt, I have observed,
10 The air is delicate.

Enter LADY MACBETH

DUNCAN
          See, see, our honored hostess!
The love that follows us sometime is our trouble,
Which still we thank as love. Herein I teach you
How you shall bid God 'ild us for your pains,
And thank us for your trouble.

LADY MACBETH
          All our service,
15 In every point twice done and then done double,
Were poor and single business to contend
Against those honors deep and broad wherewith
Your majesty loads our house. For those of old,
And the late dignities heaped up to them,
20 We rest your hermits.

ACT ONE, Scene 6

A hautboy is a loud woodwind instrument—the ancestor of the modern oboe—used in outdoor ceremonies.

The stage is lit by torches. Hautboys play. DUNCAN *enters, together with* MALCOLM, DONALBAIN, BANQUO, LENNOX, MACDUFF, ROSS, ANGUS, *and their attendants.*

DUNCAN

This castle is in a pleasant place. The air is sweet and appeals to my refined senses.

BANQUO

The fact that this summer bird, the house martin, builds his nests here proves how inviting the breezes are. There isn't a single protrusion in the castle walls where these birds haven't built their hanging nests to sleep and breed. I've noticed that they always like to settle and mate where the air is the nicest.

LADY MACBETH *enters.*

DUNCAN

Look, here comes our honored hostess! Sometimes the love my subjects bring me is inconvenient, but I still accept it as love. In doing so, I'm teaching you to thank me for the incovenience I'm causing you by being here, because it comes from my love to you.

LADY MACBETH

Everything we're doing for you, even if it were doubled and then doubled again, is nothing compared to the honors you have brought to our family. We gladly welcome you as our guests, with gratitude for both the honors you've given us before and the new honors you've just given us.

DUNCAN
                                 Where's the thane of Cawdor?
We coursed him at the heels and had a purpose
To be his purveyor; but he rides well,
And his great love, sharp as his spur, hath holp him
To his home before us. Fair and noble hostess,

25   We are your guest tonight.

LADY MACBETH
                                     Your servants ever
Have theirs, themselves, and what is theirs in compt,
To make their audit at your highness' pleasure,
Still to return your own.

DUNCAN
                           Give me your hand.
Conduct me to mine host. We love him highly

30   And shall continue our graces towards him.
By your leave, hostess.
                                         Exeun

DUNCAN

Where is Macbeth, the thane of Cawdor? We followed closely after him. I hoped to arrive here before him, but he rides swiftly. And his great love, which is as sharp as his spur, helped him beat us here. Fair and noble hostess, we are your guests tonight.

LADY MACBETH

We are your servants, your highness, and as always our house and everything in it is at your disposal, for after all, we keep it in your trust and we're glad to give you back what's yours.

DUNCAN

Give me your hand. Bring me to my host, Macbeth. I love him dearly, and I shall continue to favor him. Whenever you're ready, hostess.

They all exit.

ACT ONE, Scene 7

*Hautboys. Torches. Enter a sewer and divers servants with
dishes and service over the stage. Then enter* MACBETH

MACBETH

If it were done when 'tis done, then 'twere well
It were done quickly. If the assassination
Could trammel up the consequence, and catch
With his surcease success; that but this blow
5   Might be the be-all and the end-all here,
But here, upon this bank and shoal of time,
We'd jump the life to come. But in these cases
We still have judgment here, that we but teach
Bloody instructions, which, being taught, return
10   To plague th' inventor: this even-handed justice
Commends the ingredients of our poisoned chalice
To our own lips. He's here in double trust:
First, as I am his kinsman and his subject,
Strong both against the deed; then, as his host,
15   Who should against his murderer shut the door,
Not bear the knife myself. Besides, this Duncan
Hath borne his faculties so meek, hath been
So clear in his great office, that his virtues
Will plead like angels, trumpet-tongued, against
20   The deep damnation of his taking-off;
And pity, like a naked newborn babe,
Striding the blast, or heaven's cherubim, horsed
Upon the sightless couriers of the air,
Shall blow the horrid deed in every eye,
25   That tears shall drown the wind. I have no spur
To prick the sides of my intent, but only
Vaulting ambition, which o'erleaps itself
And falls on th' other.

ACT ONE, Scene 7

Hautboys play. The stage is lit by torches. A butler enters, and various servants carry utensils and dishes of food across the stage. Then MACBETH *enters.*

MACBETH

If this business would really be finished when I did the deed, then it would be best to get it over with quickly. If the assassination of the king could work like a net, sweeping up everything and preventing any consequences, then the murder would be the be-all and end-all of the whole affair, and I would gladly put my soul and the afterlife at risk to do it. But for crimes like these there are still punishments in this world. By committing violent crimes we only teach other people to commit violence, and the violence of our students will come back to plague us teachers. Justice, being equal to everyone, forces us to drink from the poisoned cup that we serve to others. The king trusts me in two ways. First of all, I am his kinsman and his subject, so I should always try to protect him. Second, I am his host, so I should be closing the door in his murderer's face, not trying to murder him myself. Besides, Duncan has been such a humble leader, so free of corruption, that his virtuous legacy will speak for him when he dies, as if angels were playing trumpets against the injustice of his murder. Pity, like an innocent newborn baby, will ride the wind with winged angels on invisible horses through the air to spread news of the horrible deed to everyone everywhere. People will shed a flood of tears that will drown the wind like a horrible downpour of rain. I can't spur myself to action. The only thing motivating me is ambition, which makes people rush ahead of themselves toward disaster.

Enter LADY MACBETH

How now! What news?

LADY MACBETH
He has almost supped. Why have you left the chamber?

MACBETH
30   Hath he asked for me?

LADY MACBETH
Know you not he has?

MACBETH
We will proceed no further in this business.
He hath honored me of late, and I have bought
Golden opinions from all sorts of people,
Which would be worn now in their newest gloss,
35   Not cast aside so soon.

LADY MACBETH
Was the hope drunk
Wherein you dressed yourself? Hath it slept since?
And wakes it now, to look so green and pale
At what it did so freely? From this time
Such I account thy love. Art thou afeard
40   To be the same in thine own act and valor
As thou art in desire? Wouldst thou have that
Which thou esteem'st the ornament of life,
And live a coward in thine own esteem,
Letting "I dare not" wait upon "I would,"
45   Like the poor cat i' th' adage?

MACBETH
Prithee, peace:
I dare do all that may become a man;
Who dares do more is none.

LADY MACBETH
What beast was 't, then,
That made you break this enterprise to me?
When you durst do it, then you were a man;

LADY MACBETH *enters.*

What news do you have?

LADY MACBETH
He has almost finished dinner. Why did you leave the dining room?

MACBETH
Has he asked for me?

LADY MACBETH
Don't you know he has?

MACBETH
We can't go on with this plan. The king has just honored me, and I have earned the good opinion of all sorts of people. I want to enjoy these honors while the feeling is fresh and not throw them away so soon.

LADY MACBETH
Were you drunk when you seemed so hopeful before? Have you gone to sleep and woken up green and pale in fear of this idea? From now on this is what I'll think of your love. Are you afraid to act the way you desire? Will you take the crown you want so badly, or will you live as a coward, always saying "I can't" after you say "I want to"? You're like the poor cat in the old story.

MACBETH
Please, stop! I dare to do only what is proper for a man to do. He who dares to do more is not a man at all.

LADY MACBETH
If you weren't a man, then what kind of animal were you when you first told me you wanted to do this? When you dared to do it, that's when you were a man.

50 And to be more than what you were, you would
Be so much more the man. Nor time nor place
Did then adhere, and yet you would make both.
They have made themselves, and that their fitness now
Does unmake you. I have given suck, and know
55 How tender 'tis to love the babe that milks me.
I would, while it was smiling in my face,
Have plucked my nipple from his boneless gums
And dashed the brains out, had I so sworn as you
Have done to this.

MACBETH
If we should fail?

LADY MACBETH
We fail?
60 But screw your courage to the sticking-place,
And we'll not fail. When Duncan is asleep—
Whereto the rather shall his day's hard journey
Soundly invite him—his two chamberlains
Will I with wine and wassail so convince
65 That memory, the warder of the brain,
Shall be a fume, and the receipt of reason
A limbeck only: when in swinish sleep
Their drenchèd natures lie as in a death,
What cannot you and I perform upon
70 The unguarded Duncan? What not put upon
His spongy officers, who shall bear the guilt
Of our great quell?

MACBETH
Bring forth men-children only,
For thy undaunted mettle should compose
Nothing but males. Will it not be received,
75 When we have marked with blood those sleepy two
Of his own chamber and used their very daggers,
That they have done 't?

And if you go one step further by doing what you dared to do before, you'll be that much more the man. The time and place weren't right before, but you would have gone ahead with the murder anyhow. Now the time and place are just right, but they're almost too good for you. I have suckled a baby, and I know how sweet it is to love the baby at my breast. But even as the baby was smiling up at me, I would have plucked my nipple out of its mouth and smashed its brains out against a wall if I had sworn to do that the same way you have sworn to do this.

MACBETH
But if we fail—

LADY MACBETH
We, fail? If you get your courage up, we can't fail. When Duncan is asleep—the day's hard journey has definitely made him tired—I'll get his two servants so drunk that their memory will go up in smoke through the chimneys of their brains. When they lie asleep like pigs, so drunk they'll be dead to the world, what won't you and I be able to do to the unguarded Duncan? And whatever we do, we can lay all the blame on the drunken servants.

MACBETH
May you only give birth to male children, because your fearless spirit should create nothing that isn't masculine. Once we have covered the two servants with blood, and used their daggers to kill, won't people believe that they were the culprits?

LADY MACBETH
                              Who dares receive it other,
          As we shall make our griefs and clamor roar
          Upon his death?

MACBETH
                              I am settled, and bend up
80   Each corporal agent to this terrible feat.
          Away, and mock the time with fairest show.
          False face must hide what the false heart doth know.

                                                    Exeunt

LADY MACBETH
Who could think it happened any other way? We'll be grieving loudly when we hear that Duncan has died.

MACBETH
Now I'm decided, and I will exert every muscle in my body to commit this crime. Go now, and pretend to be a friendly hostess. Hide with a false pleasant face what you know in your false, evil heart.

They exit.

ACT II

Scene 1

Enter BANQUO, *and* FLEANCE, *with a torch before him*

BANQUO
How goes the night, boy?

FLEANCE
The moon is down. I have not heard the clock.

BANQUO
And she goes down at twelve.

FLEANCE
               I take 't 'tis later, sir.

BANQUO
Hold, take my sword. There's husbandry in heaven;
5 Their candles are all out. Take thee that too.
A heavy summons lies like lead upon me,
And yet I would not sleep. Merciful powers,
Restrain in me the cursèd thoughts that nature
Gives way to in repose.

Enter MACBETH *and a* SERVANT *with a torch*

            Give me my sword. Who's there?

MACBETH
10 A friend.

BANQUO
What, sir, not yet at rest? The king's a-bed.
He hath been in unusual pleasure, and
Sent forth great largess to your offices.
This diamond he greets your wife withal,
15 By the name of most kind hostess, and shut up
In measureless content.

MACBETH
            Being unprepared,
Our will became the servant to defect,

ACT II

Scene 1

BANQUO *enters with* FLEANCE, *who lights the way with a torch.*

BANQUO

How's the night going, boy?

FLEANCE

The moon has set. The clock hasn't struck yet.

BANQUO

The moon sets at twelve, right?

FLEANCE

I think it's later than that, sir.

BANQUO

Here, take my sword. The heavens are being stingy with their light. Take this, too. I'm tired and feeling heavy, but I can't sleep. Merciful powers, keep away the nightmares that plague me when I rest!

MACBETH *enters with a* SERVANT, *who carries a torch.*

Give me my sword. Who's there?

MACBETH

A friend.

BANQUO

You're not asleep yet, sir? The king's in bed. He's been in an unusually good mood and has granted many gifts to your household and servants. This diamond is a present from him to your wife for her boundless hospitality. *(he hands* MACBETH *a diamond)*

MACBETH

Because we were unprepared for the king's visit, we

Which else should free have wrought.

BANQUO
                                    All's well.
I dreamt last night of the three weird sisters:
20   To you they have showed some truth.

MACBETH
                                    I think not of them.
Yet, when we can entreat an hour to serve,
We would spend it in some words upon that business,
If you would grant the time.

BANQUO
                              At your kind'st leisure.

MACBETH
If you shall cleave to my consent, when 'tis,
25   It shall make honor for you.

BANQUO
                              So I lose none
In seeking to augment it, but still keep
My bosom franchised and allegiance clear,
I shall be counselled.

MACBETH
Good repose the while!

BANQUO
30   Thanks, sir: the like to you!

                        Exeunt BANQUO *and* FLEANCE

MACBETH
(to the SERVANT*)* Go bid thy mistress, when my drink is ready,
She strike upon the bell. Get thee to bed.

                              Exit SERVANT

Is this a dagger which I see before me,
The handle toward my hand? Come, let me clutch thee.

weren't able to entertain him as well as we would have wanted to.

BANQUO

Everything's OK. I had a dream last night about the three witches. At least part of what they said about you was true.

MACBETH

I don't think about them now. But when we have an hour to spare we can talk more about it, if you're willing.

BANQUO

Whenever you like.

MACBETH

If you stick with me, when the time comes, there will be something in it for you.

BANQUO

I'll do whatever you say, as long as I can do it with a clear conscience.

MACBETH

Rest easy in the meantime.

BANQUO

Thank you, sir. You do the same.

BANQUO *and* FLEANCE *exit.*

MACBETH

(to the SERVANT*)* Go and tell your mistress to strike the bell when my drink is ready. Get yourself to bed.

The SERVANT *exits.*

Is this a dagger I see in front of me, with its handle pointing toward my hand? *(to the dagger)* Come, let me hold you. *(he grabs at the air in front of him without*

35 I have thee not, and yet I see thee still.
Art thou not, fatal vision, sensible
To feeling as to sight? Or art thou but
A dagger of the mind, a false creation,
Proceeding from the heat-oppressèd brain?
40 I see thee yet, in form as palpable
As this which now I draw.
Thou marshall'st me the way that I was going,
And such an instrument I was to use.
Mine eyes are made the fools o' th' other senses,
45 Or else worth all the rest. I see thee still,
And on thy blade and dudgeon gouts of blood,
Which was not so before. There's no such thing.
It is the bloody business which informs
Thus to mine eyes. Now o'er the one half-world
50 Nature seems dead, and wicked dreams abuse
The curtained sleep. Witchcraft celebrates
Pale Hecate's offerings, and withered murder,
Alarumed by his sentinel, the wolf,
Whose howl's his watch, thus with his stealthy pace,
55 With Tarquin's ravishing strides, towards his design
Moves like a ghost. Thou sure and firm-set earth,
Hear not my steps, which way they walk, for fear
Thy very stones prate of my whereabout,
And take the present horror from the time,
60 Which now suits with it. Whiles I threat, he lives.
Words to the heat of deeds too cold breath gives.

A bell rings

I go, and it is done. The bell invites me.
Hear it not, Duncan, for it is a knell
That summons thee to heaven or to hell.

            Exit

touching anything) I don't have you but I can still see
you. Fateful apparition, isn't it possible to touch you
as well as see you? Or are you nothing more than a
dagger created by the mind, a hallucination from my
fevered brain? I can still see you, and you look as real
as this other dagger that I'm pulling out now. *(he
draws a dagger)* You're leading me toward the place I
was going already, and I was planning to use a weapon
just like you. My eyesight must either be the one sense
that's not working, or else it's the only one that's working right. I can still see you, and I see blood splotches
on your blade and handle that weren't there before. *(to
himself)* There's no dagger here. It's the murder I'm
about to do that's making me think I see one. Now half
the world is asleep and being deceived by evil nightmares. Witches are offering sacrifices to their goddess
Hecate. Old man murder, having been roused by the
howls of his wolf, walks silently to his destination,
moving like Tarquin, as quiet as a ghost. *(speaking to
the ground)* Hard ground, don't listen to the direction
of my steps. I don't want you to echo back where I am
and break the terrible stillness of this moment, a
silence that is so appropriate for what I'm about to do.
While I stay here talking, Duncan lives. The more I
talk, the more my courage cools.

Tarquin was a Roman prince who sneaked into a Roman wife's bedroom in the middle of the night and raped her.

A bell rings.

I'm going now. The murder is as good as done. The bell
is telling me to do it. Don't listen to the bell, Duncan,
because it summons you either to heaven or to hell.

MACBETH *exits.*

ACT TWO, Scene 2

Enter LADY MACBETH

LADY MACBETH
That which hath made them drunk hath made me bold.
What hath quenched them hath given me fire.
Hark! Peace! It was the owl that shrieked, the fatal bellman,
Which gives the stern'st good-night. He is about it.
5   The doors are open, and the surfeited grooms
Do mock their charge with snores. I have drugged their possets,
That death and nature do contend about them,
Whether they live or die.

MACBETH
(within)   Who's there? What, ho!

LADY MACBETH
Alack, I am afraid they have awaked,
10   And 'tis not done. Th' attempt and not the deed
Confounds us. Hark! I laid their daggers ready;
He could not miss 'em. Had he not resembled
My father as he slept, I had done 't.

Enter MACBETH, *with bloody daggers*

                   My husband!

MACBETH
I have done the deed. Didst thou not hear a noise?

LADY MACBETH
15   I heard the owl scream and the crickets cry.
Did not you speak?

MACBETH
          When?

ACT TWO, Scene 2

LADY MACBETH *enters.*

LADY MACBETH
The alcohol that got the servants drunk has made me bold. The same liquor that quenched their thirst has fired me up. Listen! Quiet! That was the owl that shrieked, with a scary "good night" like the bells they ring before they execute people. Macbeth must be killing the king right now. The doors to Duncan's chamber are open, and the drunk servants make a mockery of their jobs by snoring instead of protecting the king. I put so many drugs in their drinks that you can't tell if they're alive or dead.

MACBETH
(from offstage) Who's there? What is it?

LADY MACBETH
Oh no, I'm afraid the servants woke up, and the murder didn't happen. For us to attempt murder and not succeed would ruin us. *(She hears a noise.)* Listen to that! I put the servants' daggers where Macbeth would find them. He couldn't have missed them. If Duncan hadn't reminded me of my father when I saw him sleeping, I would have killed him myself.

MACBETH *enters carrying bloody daggers.*

My husband!

MACBETH
I have done the deed. Did you hear a noise?

LADY MACBETH
I heard the owl scream and the crickets cry. Didn't you say something?

MACBETH
When?

LADY MACBETH
                              Now.

MACBETH
                                        As I descended?

LADY MACBETH
Ay.

MACBETH
        Hark! Who lies i' th' second chamber?

LADY MACBETH
Donalbain.

MACBETH
(looking at his hands) This is a sorry sight.

LADY MACBETH
A foolish thought, to say a sorry sight.

MACBETH
20   There's one did laugh in 's sleep, and one cried. "Murder!"
That they did wake each other. I stood and heard them.
But they did say their prayers, and addressed them
Again to sleep.

LADY MACBETH
                        There are two lodged together.

MACBETH
One cried, "God bless us!" and "Amen" the other,
25   As they had seen me with these hangman's hands.
List'ning their fear I could not say "Amen,"
When they did say "God bless us!"

LADY MACBETH
Consider it not so deeply.

MACBETH
But wherefore could not I pronounce "Amen"?
30   I had most need of blessing, and "Amen"
Stuck in my throat.

LADY MACBETH
                        These deeds must not be thought
After these ways. So, it will make us mad.

LADY MACBETH
Just now.

MACBETH
As I came down?

LADY MACBETH
Yes.

MACBETH
Listen! Who's sleeping in the second chamber?

LADY MACBETH
Donalbain.

MACBETH
(looking at his bloody hands) This is a sorry sight.

LADY MACBETH
That's a stupid thing to say.

MACBETH
One of the servants laughed in his sleep, and one cried, "Murder!" and they woke each other up. I stood and listened to them, but then they said their prayers and went back to sleep.

LADY MACBETH
Malcolm and Donalbain are asleep in the same room.

MACBETH
One servant cried, "God bless us!" and the other replied, "Amen," as if they had seen my bloody hands. Listening to their frightened voices, I couldn't reply "Amen" when they said "God bless us!"

LADY MACBETH
Don't think about it so much.

MACBETH
But why couldn't I say "Amen"? I desperately needed God's blessing, but the word "Amen" stuck in my throat.

LADY MACBETH
We can't think that way about what we did. If we do, it'll drive us crazy.

MACBETH
Methought I heard a voice cry, "Sleep no more!
Macbeth does murder sleep"—the innocent sleep,
35   Sleep that knits up the raveled sleave of care,
The death of each day's life, sore labor's bath,
Balm of hurt minds, great nature's second course,
Chief nourisher in life's feast.

LADY MACBETH
                                    What do you mean?

MACBETH
Still it cried, "Sleep no more!" to all the house.
40   "Glamis hath murdered sleep, and therefore Cawdor
Shall sleep no more. Macbeth shall sleep no more."

LADY MACBETH
Who was it that thus cried? Why, worthy thane,
You do unbend your noble strength to think
So brainsickly of things. Go get some water,
45   And wash this filthy witness from your hand.
Why did you bring these daggers from the place?
They must lie there. Go carry them and smear
The sleepy grooms with blood.

MACBETH
                                    I'll go no more:
I am afraid to think what I have done;
50   Look on 't again I dare not.

LADY MACBETH
                                    Infirm of purpose!
Give me the daggers. The sleeping and the dead
Are but as pictures. 'Tis the eye of childhood
That fears a painted devil. If he do bleed,
I'll gild the faces of the grooms withal,
55   For it must seem their guilt.

                                                        Exit

Knock within

MACBETH

I thought I heard a voice cry, "Sleep no more! Macbeth is murdering sleep." Innocent sleep. Sleep that soothes away all our worries. Sleep that puts each day to rest. Sleep that relieves the weary laborer and heals hurt minds. Sleep, the main course in life's feast, and the most nourishing.

LADY MACBETH

What are you talking about?

MACBETH

The voice kept crying, "Sleep no more!" to everyone in the house. "Macbeth has murdered sleep, and therefore Macbeth will sleep no more."

LADY MACBETH

Who said that? Why, my worthy lord, you let yourself become weak when you think about things in this cowardly way. Go get some water and wash this bloody evidence from your hands. Why did you carry these daggers out of the room? They have to stay there. Go take them back and smear the sleeping guards with the blood.

MACBETH

I can't go back. I'm afraid even to think about what I've done. I can't stand to look at it again.

LADY MACBETH

Coward! Give me the daggers. Dead and sleeping people can't hurt you any more than pictures can. Only children are afraid of scary pictures. If Duncan bleeds I'll paint the servants' faces with his blood. We must make it seem like they're guilty.

LADY MACBETH exits.

A sound of knocking from offstage.

ACT TWO

MACBETH
                              Whence is that knocking?
How is 't with me when every noise appals me?
What hands are here? Ha! They pluck out mine eyes.
Will all great Neptune's ocean wash this blood
Clean from my hand? No, this my hand will rather
The multitudinous seas incarnadine,
60   Making the green one red.

Enter LADY MACBETH

LADY MACBETH
My hands are of your color, but I shame
To wear a heart so white.

Knock within

                              I hear a knocking
At the south entry. Retire we to our chamber.
65   A little water clears us of this deed.
How easy is it, then! Your constancy
Hath left you unattended.

Knock within

                              Hark! More knocking.
Get on your nightgown, lest occasion call us
And show us to be watchers. Be not lost
70   So poorly in your thoughts.
MACBETH
To know my deed, 'twere best not know myself.

Knock within

Wake Duncan with thy knocking. I would thou couldst.
                              Exeunt

MACBETH

Where is that knocking coming from? What's happening to me, that I'm frightened of every noise? *(looking at his hands)* Whose hands are these? Ha! They're plucking out my eyes. Will all the water in the ocean wash this blood from my hands? No, instead my hands will stain the seas scarlet, turning the green waters red.

LADY MACBETH *enters.*

LADY MACBETH

My hands are as red as yours, but I would be ashamed if my heart were as pale and weak.

A sound of knocking from offstage.

I hear someone knocking at the south entry. Let's go back to our bedroom. A little water will wash away the evidence of our guilt. It's so simple! You've lost your resolve.

A sound of knocking from offstage.

Listen! There's more knocking. Put on your nightgown, in case someone comes and sees that we're awake. Snap out of your daze.

MACBETH

Rather than have to think about my crime, I'd prefer to be completely unconscious.

A sound of knocking from offstage.

Wake Duncan with your knocking. I wish you could!
They exit.

ACT TWO, Scene 3

Enter a PORTER. *Knocking within*

PORTER
Here's a knocking indeed! If a man were porter of hell-gate,
he should have old turning the key.

Knock within

Knock, knock, knock! Who's there, i' th' name of
Beelzebub? Here's a farmer that hanged himself on the
5   expectation of plenty. Come in time, have napkins enough
about you, here you'll sweat for 't.

Knock within

Knock, knock! Who's there, in th' other devil's name?
Faith, here's an equivocator that could swear in both the
scales against either scale, who committed treason enough
10   for God's sake, yet could not equivocate to heaven. O, come
in, equivocator.

Knock within

Knock, knock, knock! Who's there? Faith, here's an English
tailor come hither for stealing out of a French hose. Come
in, tailor. Here you may roast your goose.

Knock within

ACT TWO, Scene 3

A porter is a doorkeeper. → *A sound of knocking from offstage. A* PORTER, *who is obviously drunk, enters.*

PORTER

This is a lot of knocking! Come to think of it, if a man were in charge of opening the gates of hell to let people in, he would have to turn the key a lot.

A sound of knocking from offstage.

Knock, knock, knock! *(pretending he's the gatekeeper in hell)* Who's there, in the devil's name? Maybe it's a farmer who killed himself because grain was cheap. *(talking to the imaginary farmer)* You're here just in time! I hope you brought some handkerchiefs; you're going to sweat a lot here.

A sound of knocking from offstage.

Knock, knock! Who's there, in the other devil's name? Maybe it's some slick, two-faced con man who lied under oath. But he found out that you can't lie to God, and now he's going to hell for perjury. Come on in, con man.

A sound of knocking from offstage.

Knock, knock, knock! Who's there? Maybe it's an English tailor who liked to skimp on the fabric for people's clothes. But now that tight pants are in fashion he can't get away with it. Come on in, tailor. You can heat your iron up in here.

A sound of knocking from offstage.

15   Knock, knock! Never at quiet. What are you? But this place
        is too cold for hell. I'll devil-porter it no further. I had
        thought to have let in some of all professions that go the
        primrose way to the everlasting bonfire.

        Knock within

        Anon, anon! I pray you, remember the porter.

        Opens the gate

        Enter MACDUFF *and* LENNOX

        MACDUFF
20   Was it so late, friend, ere you went to bed,
        That you do lie so late?

        PORTER
        'Faith sir, we were carousing till the second cock. And
        drink, sir, is a great provoker of three things.

        MACDUFF
        What three things does drink especially provoke?

        PORTER
25   Marry, sir, nose-painting, sleep, and urine. Lechery, sir, it
        provokes and unprovokes. It provokes the desire, but it
        takes away the performance. Therefore, much drink may be
        said to be an equivocator with lechery. It makes him, and it
        mars him; it sets him on, and it takes him off; it persuades
30   him, and disheartens him; makes him stand to and not
        stand to; in conclusion, equivocates him in a sleep, and,
        giving him the lie, leaves him.

        MACDUFF
        I believe drink gave thee the lie last night.

Knock, knock! Never a moment of peace! Who are you? Ah, this place is too cold to be hell. I won't pretend to be the devil's porter anymore. I was going to let someone from every profession into hell.

A sound of knocking from offstage.

I'm coming, I'm coming! Please, don't forget to leave me a tip.

The PORTER *opens the gate.*

MACDUFF *and* LENNOX *enter.*

MACDUFF

Did you go to bed so late, my friend, that you're having a hard time getting up now?

PORTER

That's right sir, we were drinking until 3 A.M., and drink, sir, makes a man do three things.

MACDUFF

What three things does drink make a man do?

PORTER

Drinking turns your nose red, it puts you to sleep, and it makes you urinate. Lust it turns on but also turns off. What I mean is, drinking stimulates desire but hinders performance. Therefore, too much drink is like a con artist when it comes to your sex drive. It sets you up for a fall. It gets you up but it keeps you from getting off. It persuades you and discourages you. It gives you an erection but doesn't let you keep it, if you see what I'm saying. It makes you dream about erotic experiences, but then it leaves you asleep and needing to pee.

MACDUFF

I believe drink did all of this to you last night.

PORTER
That it did, sir, i' th' very throat on me; but I requited him
35   for his lie, and, I think, being too strong for him, though he
took up my legs sometime, yet I made a shift to cast him.

MACDUFF
Is thy master stirring?

Enter MACBETH

Our knocking has awaked him. Here he comes.

LENNOX
Good morrow, noble sir.

MACBETH
                              Good morrow, both.

MACDUFF
40   Is the king stirring, worthy thane?

MACBETH
                                   Not yet.

MACDUFF
He did command me to call timely on him.
I have almost slipped the hour.

MACBETH
                                   I'll bring you to him.

MACDUFF
I know this is a joyful trouble to you,
But yet 'tis one.

MACBETH
45   The labor we delight in physics pain.
This is the door.

MACDUFF
                         I'll make so bold to call,
For 'tis my limited service.
                                        Exit MACDUFF

LENNOX
Goes the king hence today?

PORTER

It did, sir. It got me right in the throat. But I got even with drink. I was too strong for it. Although it weakened my legs and made me unsteady, I managed to vomit it out and laid it flat on the ground.

MACDUFF

Is your master awake?

MACBETH *enters.*

Our knocking woke him up. Here he comes.

LENNOX

Good morning, noble sir.

MACBETH

Good morning to both of you.

MACDUFF

Is the king awake, worthy thane?

MACBETH

Not yet.

MACDUFF

He commanded me to wake him up early. I've almost missed the time he requested.

MACBETH

I'll bring you to him.

MACDUFF

I know the burden of hosting him is both an honor and a trouble, but that doesn't mean it's not a trouble just the same.

MACBETH

The work we enjoy is not really work. This is the door.

MACDUFF

I'll wake him, because that's my job.

MACDUFF *exits.*

LENNOX

Is the king leaving here today?

MACBETH
He does. He did appoint so.

LENNOX
The night has been unruly. Where we lay,
50   Our chimneys were blown down and, as they say,
Lamentings heard i' th' air, strange screams of death,
And prophesying with accents terrible
Of dire combustion and confused events
New hatched to the woeful time. The obscure bird
55   Clamored the livelong night. Some say the Earth
Was feverous and did shake.

MACBETH
'Twas a rough night.

LENNOX
My young remembrance cannot parallel
A fellow to it.

Enter **MACDUFF**

MACDUFF
O horror, horror, horror!
Tongue nor heart cannot conceive nor name thee!

MACBETH & LENNOX
60   What's the matter?

MACDUFF
Confusion now hath made his masterpiece.
Most sacrilegious murder hath broke ope
The Lord's anointed temple, and stole thence
The life o' th' building!

MACBETH
What is 't you say? "The life"?

LENNOX
65   Mean you his majesty?

MACBETH

He is. He told us to arrange it.

LENNOX

The night has been chaotic. The wind blew down through the chimneys where we were sleeping. People are saying they heard cries of grief in the air, strange screams of death, and terrible voices predicting catastrophes that will usher in a woeful new age. The owl made noise all night. Some people say that the earth shook as if it had a fever.

MACBETH

It was a rough night.

LENNOX

I'm too young to remember anything like it.

MACDUFF *enters, upset.*

MACDUFF

Oh, horror, horror, horror! This is beyond words and beyond belief!

MACBETH & LENNOX

What's the matter?

MACDUFF

The worst thing imaginable has happened. A murderer has broken into God's temple and stolen the life out of it.

Macduff compares Duncan's corpse to a church that has been broken into, which confuses his listeners.

MACBETH

What are you talking about? "The life"?

LENNOX

Do you mean the king?

MACDUFF
Approach the chamber, and destroy your sight
With a new Gorgon. Do not bid me speak.
See, and then speak yourselves.

Exeunt MACBETH *and* LENNOX

                              Awake, awake!
Ring the alarum bell. Murder and treason!
70   Banquo and Donalbain! Malcolm! Awake!
Shake off this downy sleep, death's counterfeit,
And look on death itself! Up, up, and see
The great doom's image! Malcolm! Banquo!
As from your graves rise up, and walk like sprites,
75   To countenance this horror! Ring the bell.

Bell rings. Enter LADY MACBETH

LADY MACBETH
What's the business,
That such a hideous trumpet calls to parley
The sleepers of the house? Speak, speak!

MACDUFF
                              O gentle lady,
'Tis not for you to hear what I can speak:
80   The repetition, in a woman's ear,
Would murder as it fell.

Enter BANQUO

                              O Banquo, Banquo,
Our royal master's murdered!

LADY MACBETH
                              Woe, alas!
What, in our house?

MACDUFF

Go into the bedroom and see for yourself. What's in there will make you freeze with horror. Don't ask me to talk about it. Go look and then do the talking yourselves.

MACBETH *and* LENNOX *exit.*

Wake up, wake up! Ring the alarm bell. Murder and treason! Banquo and Donalbain, Malcolm! Wake up! Shake off sleep, which looks like death, and look at death itself! Get up, get up, and look at this image of doomsday! Malcolm! Banquo! Get up from your beds as if you were rising out of your own graves, and walk like ghosts to come witness this horror. Ring the bell.

A bell rings. LADY MACBETH *enters.*

LADY MACBETH

What's going on? Why is that terrifying trumpet calling together everyone who's sleeping in the house? Speak up and tell me!

MACDUFF

Oh gentle lady, my news isn't fit for your ears. If I repeated it to you, it would kill you as soon as you heard it.

BANQUO *enters.*

Oh Banquo, Banquo, the king has been murdered!

LADY MACBETH

How horrible! What, in our own house?

BANQUO
       Too cruel any where.
Dear Duff, I prithee, contradict thyself,
85 And say it is not so.

Enter MACBETH, LENNOX, *and* ROSS

MACBETH
Had I but died an hour before this chance,
I had lived a blessèd time, for from this instant
There's nothing serious in mortality.
All is but toys. Renown and grace is dead.
90 The wine of life is drawn, and the mere lees
Is left this vault to brag of.

Enter MALCOLM *and* DONALBAIN

DONALBAIN
What is amiss?

MACBETH
You are, and do not know 't.
The spring, the head, the fountain of your blood
95 Is stopped; the very source of it is stopped.

MACDUFF
Your royal father's murdered.

MALCOLM
       Oh, by whom?

LENNOX
Those of his chamber, as it seemed, had done 't.
Their hands and faces were all badged with blood.
So were their daggers, which unwiped we found
100 Upon their pillows. They stared, and were distracted.
No man's life was to be trusted with them.

MACBETH
Oh, yet I do repent me of my fury,
That I did kill them.

BANQUO

It would be a terrible event no matter where it happened. Dear Macduff, I beg you, tell us you were lying and say it isn't so.

MACBETH *and* LENNOX *reenter, with* ROSS.

MACBETH

If I had only died an hour before this event I could say I had lived a blessed life. Because from this moment on, there is nothing worth living for. Everything is a sick joke. The graceful and renowned king is dead. The wine of life has been poured out, and only the dregs remain.

MALCOLM *and* DONALBAIN *enter.*

DONALBAIN

What's wrong?

MACBETH

You are, but you don't know it yet. The source from which your royal blood comes has been stopped.

MACDUFF

Your royal father is murdered.

MALCOLM

Who did it?

LENNOX

It seems that the guards who were supposed to be protecting his chamber did it. Their hands and faces were all covered with blood. So were their daggers, which we found on their pillows, unwiped. They stared at us in confusion. No one's life should have been entrusted to them.

MACBETH

And yet I still regret the anger that drove me to kill them.

MACDUFF
                    Wherefore did you so?

MACBETH
Who can be wise, amazed, temp'rate, and furious,
105 Loyal and neutral, in a moment? No man.
Th' expedition of my violent love
Outrun the pauser, reason. Here lay Duncan,
His silver skin laced with his golden blood,
And his gashed stabs looked like a breach in nature
110 For ruin's wasteful entrance; there, the murderers,
Steeped in the colors of their trade, their daggers
Unmannerly breeched with gore. Who could refrain,
That had a heart to love, and in that heart
Courage to make 's love known?

LADY MACBETH
                              Help me hence, ho!

MACDUFF
115 Look to the lady.

MALCOLM
(aside to DONALBAIN*)* Why do we hold our tongues,
That most may claim this argument for ours?

DONALBAIN
(aside to MALCOLM*)* What should be spoken here, where our
          fate,
Hid in an auger-hole, may rush and seize us?
Let's away. Our tears are not yet brewed.

MALCOLM
120 *(aside to* DONALBAIN*)* Nor our strong sorrow
Upon the foot of motion.

BANQUO
                    Look to the lady.
                    Exit LADY MACBETH, *attended*

And when we have our naked frailties hid,
That suffer in exposure, let us meet
And question this most bloody piece of work,

MACDUFF

What did you do that for?

MACBETH

Is it possible to be wise, bewildered, calm, furious, loyal, and neutral all at once? Nobody can do that. The violent rage inspired by my love for Duncan caused me to act before I could think rationally and tell myself to pause. There was Duncan, his white skin all splattered with his precious blood. The gashes where the knives had cut him looked like wounds to nature itself. Then right next to him I saw the murderers, dripping with blood, their daggers rudely covered in gore. Who could have restrained himself, who loved Duncan and had the courage to act on it?

LADY MACBETH

Help me out of here, quickly!

MACDUFF

Take care of the lady.

MALCOLM

(speaking so that only DONALBAIN *can hear)* Why are we keeping quiet? The two of us have the most to say in this matter.

DONALBAIN

(speaking so that only MALCOLM *can hear)* What are we going to say here, where danger may be waiting to strike at us from anywhere? Let's get out of here. We haven't even begun to weep yet—but there will be time for that later.

MALCOLM

(speaking so that only DONALBAIN *can hear)* And the time hasn't come yet for us to turn our deep grief into action.

BANQUO

Take care of the lady.

LADY MACBETH *is carried out.*

125   To know it further. Fears and scruples shake us.
In the great hand of God I stand, and thence
Against the undivulged pretense I fight
Of treasonous malice.

MACDUFF
               And so do I.

ALL
                     So all.

MACBETH
Let's briefly put on manly readiness,
130   And meet i' th' hall together.

ALL
                  Well contented.

Exeunt all but MALCOLM *and* DONALBAIN

MALCOLM
What will you do? Let's not consort with them.
To show an unfelt sorrow is an office
Which the false man does easy. I'll to England.

DONALBAIN
To Ireland, I. Our separated fortune
135   Shall keep us both the safer. Where we are,
There's daggers in men's smiles. The near in blood,
The nearer bloody.

MALCOLM
           This murderous shaft that's shot
Hath not yet lighted, and our safest way
Is to avoid the aim. Therefore, to horse,
140   And let us not be dainty of leave-taking,
But shift away. There's warrant in that theft
Which steals itself when there's no mercy left.
                     Exeunt

When we're properly dressed for the cold, let's meet and discuss this bloody crime to see if we can figure anything out. Right now we're shaken up by fears and doubts. I'm putting myself in God's hands, and with his help I plan to fight against the secret plot that caused this treasonous murder.

MACDUFF

So will I.

ALL

So will we all.

MACBETH

Let's get dressed quickly and then meet in the hall.

ALL

Agreed.

Everyone exits except MALCOLM *and* DONALBAIN.

MALCOLM

What are you going to do? Let's not stay here with them. It's easy for a liar to pretend to feel sorrow when he actually feels none. I'm going to England.

DONALBAIN

I'll go to Ireland. We'll both be safer if we go separate ways. Wherever we go, men will smile at us while hiding daggers. Our closest relatives are the ones most likely to murder us.

MALCOLM

We haven't yet encountered that danger, and the best thing to do is avoid it entirely. With that in mind, let's get on our horses. We'd better not worry about saying polite good-byes; we should just get away quickly. There's good reason to escape when there's no mercy to be found anymore.

They exit.

ACT TWO, Scene 4

Enter ROSS *with an* OLD MAN

OLD MAN
Threescore and ten I can remember well,
Within the volume of which time I have seen
Hours dreadful and things strange, but this sore night
Hath trifled former knowings.

ROSS
                              Ha, good father,
5   Thou seest the heavens, as troubled with man's act,
Threatens his bloody stage. By th' clock 'tis day,
And yet dark night strangles the travelling lamp.
Is 't night's predominance or the day's shame
That darkness does the face of Earth entomb
10   When living light should kiss it?

OLD MAN
                                    'Tis unnatural,
Even like the deed that's done. On Tuesday last,
A falcon, tow'ring in her pride of place,
Was by a mousing owl hawked at and killed.

ROSS
And Duncan's horses—a thing most strange and certain—
15   Beauteous and swift, the minions of their race,
Turned wild in nature, broke their stalls, flung out,
Contending 'gainst obedience, as they would
Make war with mankind.

OLD MAN
                        'Tis said they eat each other.

ROSS
They did so, to th' amazement of mine eyes
20   That looked upon 't. Here comes the good Macduff.

Enter MACDUFF

ACT TWO, Scene 4

ROSS *and an* OLD MAN *enter.*

OLD MAN

I can remember the past seventy years pretty well, and in all that time I have seen dreadful hours and strange things. But last night's horrors make everything that came before seem like a joke.

ROSS

Ah yes, old man. You can see the skies. They look like they're upset about what mankind has been doing, and they're threatening the Earth with storms. The clock says it's daytime, but dark night is strangling the sun. Is it because night is so strong, or because day is so weak, that darkness covers the earth when it's supposed to be light?

OLD MAN

It's unnatural, just like the murder that has been committed. Last Tuesday a falcon was circling high in the sky, and it was caught and killed by an ordinary owl that usually goes after mice.

ROSS

And something else strange happened. Duncan's horses, which are beautiful and swift and the best of their breed, suddenly turned wild and broke out of their stalls. Refusing to be obedient as usual, they acted like they were at war with mankind.

OLD MAN

They say the horses ate each other.

ROSS

I saw it with my own eyes. It was an amazing sight. Here comes the good Macduff.

MACDUFF *enters.*

How goes the world, sir, now?

MACDUFF

                                        Why, see you not?

ROSS

Is 't known who did this more than bloody deed?

MACDUFF

Those that Macbeth hath slain.

ROSS

                                        Alas, the day!
What good could they pretend?

MACDUFF

                                        They were suborned.
25   Malcolm and Donalbain, the king's two sons,
        Are stol'n away and fled, which puts upon them
        Suspicion of the deed.

ROSS

                        'Gainst nature still!
        Thriftless ambition, that will raven up
        Thine own lives' means! Then 'tis most like
30   The sovereignty will fall upon Macbeth.

MACDUFF

        He is already named and gone to Scone
        To be invested.

ROSS

        Where is Duncan's body?

MACDUFF

        Carried to Colmekill,
35   The sacred storehouse of his predecessors,
        And guardian of their bones.

ROSS

                                        Will you to Scone?

MACDUFF

        No, cousin, I'll to Fife.

ROSS

                        Well, I will thither.

ACT TWO, SCENE 4

How are things going now?

MACDUFF

Can't you see for yourself?

ROSS

Does anyone know who committed this horrible crime?

MACDUFF

The servants Macbeth killed.

ROSS

It's too bad he killed them. What good would it have done those men to kill Duncan?

MACDUFF

They were paid to betray their master. Malcolm and Donalbain, the king's two sons, have run away and fled, which makes them the prime suspects.

ROSS

Everything about this is unnatural! What a stupid ambition, causing a son to kill the father who supports him. Then it looks like Macbeth will become king.

MACDUFF

He has already been named king and has left for Scone to be crowned.

ROSS

Where is Duncan's body?

MACDUFF

It was carried to Colmekill to be placed in the tomb of his ancestors, where their bones are kept safe.

ROSS

Are you going to Scone?

MACDUFF

No, cousin, I'm going to Fife.

ROSS

Well, I'll go to Scone.

MACDUFF
Well, may you see things well done there. Adieu,
Lest our old robes sit easier than our new!

ROSS
40   Farewell, father.

OLD MAN
God's benison go with you and with those
That would make good of bad and friends of foes.

Exeunt

MACDUFF

I hope things go well there. Good-bye! And let's hope things don't get worse.

ROSS

Farewell, old man.

OLD MAN

May God's blessing go with you and with all who turn bad into good, and enemies into friends!

They all exit.

ACT THREE

Scene 1

Enter BANQUO

BANQUO
Thou hast it now: king, Cawdor, Glamis, all,
As the weird women promised, and I fear
Thou played'st most foully for 't. Yet it was said
It should not stand in thy posterity,
5   But that myself should be the root and father
Of many kings. If there come truth from them—
As upon thee, Macbeth, their speeches shine—
Why, by the verities on thee made good,
May they not be my oracles as well,
10   And set me up in hope? But hush, no more.

Sennet sounded. Enter MACBETH, *as king,* LADY MACBETH,
as queen, LENNOX, ROSS, LORDS, LADIES, *and attendants.*

MACBETH
Here's our chief guest.
LADY MACBETH
                    If he had been forgotten,
It had been as a gap in our great feast,
And all-thing unbecoming.
MACBETH
Tonight we hold a solemn supper, sir,
15   And I'll request your presence.
BANQUO
                              Let your highness
Command upon me, to the which my duties
Are with a most indissoluble tie
Forever knit.

ACT THREE

Scene 1

BANQUO *enters.*

BANQUO

Now you have it all: you're the king, the thane of Cawdor, and the thane of Glamis, just like the weird women promised you. And I suspect you cheated to win these titles. But it was also prophesied that the crown would not go to your descendants, and that my sons and grandsons would be kings instead. If the witches tell the truth—which they did about you— maybe what they said about me will come true too. But shhh! I'll shut up now.

A trumpet plays. MACBETH *enters dressed as king, and* LADY MACBETH *enters dressed as queen, together with* LENNOX, ROSS, LORDS, LADIES, *and their attendants.*

MACBETH

(indicating BANQUO*)* Here's our most important guest.

LADY MACBETH

If we forgot him, our big celebration wouldn't be complete, and that wouldn't be any good.

MACBETH

(to BANQUO*)* Tonight we're having a ceremonial banquet, and I want you to be there.

BANQUO

Whatever your highness commands me to do, it is always my duty to do it.

MACBETH
Ride you this afternoon?

BANQUO
20   Ay, my good lord.

MACBETH
We should have else desired your good advice—
Which still hath been both grave and prosperous—
In this day's council, but we'll take tomorrow.
Is 't far you ride?

BANQUO
25   As far, my lord, as will fill up the time
'Twixt this and supper. Go not my horse the better,
I must become a borrower of the night
For a dark hour or twain.

MACBETH
                          Fail not our feast.

BANQUO
My lord, I will not.

MACBETH
30   We hear our bloody cousins are bestowed
In England and in Ireland, not confessing
Their cruel parricide, filling their hearers
With strange invention. But of that tomorrow,
When therewithal we shall have cause of state
35   Craving us jointly. Hie you to horse. Adieu,
Till your return at night. Goes Fleance with you?

BANQUO
Ay, my good lord. Our time does call upon 's.

MACBETH
I wish your horses swift and sure of foot,
And so I do commend you to their backs.
40   Farewell.

Exit BANQUO

Let every man be master of his time
Till seven at night. To make society
The sweeter welcome, we will keep ourself
Till suppertime alone. While then, God be with you!

MACBETH

Are you going riding this afternoon?

BANQUO

Yes, my good lord.

MACBETH

We would have liked to have heard your good advice, which has always been serious and helpful, at the council today, but we'll wait until tomorrow. Are you riding far?

BANQUO

I'm going far enough that I'll be riding from now until dinner. Unless my horse goes faster than expected, I will be back an hour or two after sunset.

MACBETH

Don't miss our feast.

BANQUO

My lord, I won't miss it.

MACBETH

We hear that the princes, those murderers, have hidden in England and Ireland. They haven't confessed to cruelly murdering their own father, and they've been making up strange lies to tell their hosts. But we can talk more about that tomorrow, when we'll discuss matters of state that concern us both. Hurry up and get to your horse. Good-bye, until you return tonight. Is Fleance going with you?

BANQUO

Yes, my good lord. It's time we hit the road.

MACBETH

I hope your horses are fast and surefooted. And with that, I send you to them. Farewell.

                               BANQUO *exits.*

Everybody may do as they please until seven o'clock tonight. In order to make your company even more enjoyable, I'm going to keep to myself until suppertime. Until then, God be with you!

Exeunt all except MACBETH *and a* SERVANT

45   Sirrah, a word with you. Attend those men
        Our pleasure?

SERVANT
        They are, my lord, without the palace gate.

MACBETH
        Bring them before us.

                                    Exit SERVANT

                    To be thus is nothing,
        But to be safely thus. Our fears in Banquo
50   Stick deep, and in his royalty of nature
        Reigns that which would be feared. 'Tis much he dares,
        And to that dauntless temper of his mind
        He hath a wisdom that doth guide his valor
        To act in safety. There is none but he
55   Whose being I do fear, and under him
        My genius is rebuked, as it is said
        Mark Antony's was by Caesar. He chid the sisters
        When first they put the name of king upon me
        And bade them speak to him. Then, prophetlike,
60   They hailed him father to a line of kings.
        Upon my head they placed a fruitless crown
        And put a barren scepter in my grip,
        Thence to be wrenched with an unlineal hand,
        No son of mine succeeding. If 't be so,
65   For Banquo's issue have I filed my mind;
        For them the gracious Duncan have I murdered;
        Put rancors in the vessel of my peace
        Only for them; and mine eternal jewel
        Given to the common enemy of man,
70   To make them kings, the seed of Banquo kings!
        Rather than so, come fate into the list,
        And champion me to th' utterance. Who's there?

        Enter SERVANT *and two* MURDERERS

Everyone exits except MACBETH *and a* SERVANT.
(to the SERVANT*)* You there, let me have a word with you. Are those men waiting for me?

SERVANT
They're waiting outside the palace gate, my lord.

MACBETH
Bring them to me.

The SERVANT *exits.*
To be the king is nothing if I'm not safe as the king. I'm very afraid of Banquo. There's something noble about him that makes me fear him. He's willing to take risks, and his mind never stops working. He has the wisdom to act bravely but also safely. I'm not afraid of anyone but him. Around him, my guardian angel is frightened, just as Mark Antony's angel supposedly feared Octavius Caesar. Banquo chided the witches when they first called me king, asking them to tell him his own future. Then, like prophets, they named him the father to a line of kings. They gave me a crown and a scepter that I can't pass on. Someone outside my family will take these things away from me, since no son of mine will take my place as king. If this is true, then I've tortured my conscience and murdered the gracious Duncan for Banquo's sons. I've ruined my own peace for their benefit. I've handed over my ever-lasting soul to the devil so that they could be kings. Banquo's sons, kings! Instead of watching that happen, I will challenge fate to battle and fight to the death. Who's there!

The SERVANT *comes back in with two* MURDERERS.

Now go to the door and stay there till we call.

Exit SERVANT

Was it not yesterday we spoke together?

FIRST MURDERER

75   It was, so please your highness.

MACBETH

Well then, now
Have you considered of my speeches? Know
That it was he, in the times past, which held you
So under fortune, which you thought had been
Our innocent self. This I made good to you

80   In our last conference, passed in probation with you,
How you were borne in hand, how crossed, the instruments,
Who wrought with them, and all things else that might
To half a soul and to a notion crazed
Say, "Thus did Banquo."

FIRST MURDERER

You made it known to us.

MACBETH

85   I did so, and went further, which is now
Our point of second meeting. Do you find
Your patience so predominant in your nature
That you can let this go? Are you so gospeled
To pray for this good man and for his issue,

90   Whose heavy hand hath bowed you to the grave
And beggared yours forever?

FIRST MURDERER

We are men, my liege.

MACBETH

Ay, in the catalogue ye go for men,
As hounds and greyhounds, mongrels, spaniels, curs,
Shoughs, water-rugs, and demi-wolves are clept

95   All by the name of dogs. The valued file
Distinguishes the swift, the slow, the subtle,
The housekeeper, the hunter, every one
According to the gift which bounteous nature
Hath in him closed, whereby he does receive

Now go to the door and stay there until I call for you.

The SERVANT *exits.*

Wasn't it just yesterday that we spoke to each other?

FIRST MURDERER

It was yesterday, your highness.

MACBETH

Well, did you think about what I said? You should know that it was Banquo who made your lives hell for so long, which you always thought was my fault. But I was innocent. I showed you the proof at our last meeting. I explained how you were deceived, how you were thwarted, the things that were used against you, who was working against you, and a lot of other things that would convince even a half-wit or a crazy person to say, "Banquo did it!"

FIRST MURDERER

You explained it all.

MACBETH

I did that and more, which brings me to the point of this second meeting. Are you so patient and forgiving that you're going to let him off the hook? Are you so pious that you would pray for this man and his children, a man who has pushed you toward an early grave and put your family in poverty forever?

FIRST MURDERER

We are men, my lord.

MACBETH

Yes, you're part of the species called men. Just as hounds and greyhounds, mongrels, spaniels, mutts, shaggy lapdogs, swimming dogs, and wolf-dog cross-breeds are all dogs. But if you list the different kinds of dogs according to their qualities, you can distinguish which breeds are fast or slow, which ones are clever, which ones are watchdogs, and which ones hunters. You can classify each dog according to the

ACT THREE

100   Particular addition, from the bill
That writes them all alike. And so of men.
Now, if you have a station in the file,
Not i' th' worst rank of manhood, say 't,
And I will put that business in your bosoms,
105   Whose execution takes your enemy off,
Grapples you to the heart and love of us,
Who wear our health but sickly in his life,
Which in his death were perfect.

SECOND MURDERER
                              I am one, my liege,
Whom the vile blows and buffets of the world
110   Have so incensed that I am reckless what
I do to spite the world.

FIRST MURDERER
                        And I another
So weary with disasters, tugged with fortune,
That I would set my life on any chance,
To mend it or be rid on 't.

MACBETH
                          Both of you
115   Know Banquo was your enemy.

BOTH MURDERERS
                            True, my lord.

MACBETH
So is he mine; and in such bloody distance
That every minute of his being thrusts
Against my near'st of life. And though I could
With barefaced power sweep him from my sight
120   And bid my will avouch it, yet I must not,
For certain friends that are both his and mine,
Whose loves I may not drop, but wail his fall
Who I myself struck down. And thence it is,
That I to your assistance do make love,
125   Masking the business from the common eye
For sundry weighty reasons.

natural gifts that separate it from all other dogs. It's the same with men. Now, if you occupy some place in the list of men that isn't down at the very bottom, tell me. Because if that's the case, I will tell you a plan that will get rid of your enemy and bring you closer to me. As long as Banquo lives, I am sick. I'll be healthy when he is dead.

SECOND MURDERER
My lord, I've been so kicked around by the world, and I'm so angry, that I don't even care what I do.

FIRST MURDERER
I'm the same. I'm so sick of bad luck and trouble that I'd risk my life on any bet, as long as it would either fix my life or end it once and for all.

MACBETH
You both know Banquo was your enemy.

BOTH MURDERERS
It's true, my lord.

MACBETH
He's my enemy too, and I hate him so much that every minute he's alive it eats away at my heart. Since I'm king, I could simply use my power to get rid of him. But I can't do that, because he and I have friends in common whom I need, so I have to be able to moan and cry over his death in public even though I'll be the one who had him killed. That's why I need your help right now. I have to hide my real plans from the public eye for many important reasons.

SECOND MURDERER
                              We shall, my lord,
Perform what you command us.

FIRST MURDERER
                                        Though our lives—

MACBETH
Your spirits shine through you. Within this hour at most
I will advise you where to plant yourselves,
130   Acquaint you with the perfect spy o' th' time,
The moment on 't; for 't must be done tonight,
And something from the palace; always thought
That I require a clearness. And with him—
To leave no rubs nor botches in the work—
135   Fleance, his son, that keeps him company,
Whose absence is no less material to me
Than is his father's, must embrace the fate
Of that dark hour. Resolve yourselves apart.
I'll come to you anon.

BOTH MURDERERS
                              We are resolved, my lord.

MACBETH
140   I'll call upon you straight. Abide within.
                                        Exeunt **MURDERERS**
It is concluded. Banquo, thy soul's flight,
If it find heaven, must find it out tonight.
                                                  Exit

SECOND MURDERER
We'll do what you want us to, my lord.

FIRST MURDERER
Though our lives—

MACBETH
(interrupts him) I can see the determination in your eyes. Within the next hour I'll tell you where to go and exactly when to strike. It must be done tonight, away from the palace. Always remember that I must be free from suspicion. For the plan to work perfectly, you must kill both Banquo and his son, Fleance, who keeps him company. Getting rid of Fleance is as important to me as knocking off Banquo. Each of you should make up your own mind about whether you're going to do this. I'll come to you soon.

BOTH MURDERERS
We have decided, my lord. We're in.

MACBETH
I'll call for you soon. Stay inside.
                              The MURDERERS *exit.*
The deal is closed. Banquo, if your soul is going to make it to heaven, tonight's the night.
                              He exits.

ACT THREE, Scene 2

Enter LADY MACBETH *and a* SERVANT

LADY MACBETH
Is Banquo gone from court?

SERVANT
Ay, madam, but returns again tonight.

LADY MACBETH
Say to the king I would attend his leisure
For a few words.

SERVANT
5   Madam, I will.

Exit SERVANT

LADY MACBETH
Naught's had, all's spent,
Where our desire is got without content.
'Tis safer to be that which we destroy
Than by destruction dwell in doubtful joy.

Enter MACBETH

10   How now, my lord! Why do you keep alone,
Of sorriest fancies your companions making,
Using those thoughts which should indeed have died
With them they think on? Things without all remedy
Should be without regard. What's done is done.

MACBETH
15   We have scorched the snake, not killed it.
She'll close and be herself whilst our poor malice
Remains in danger of her former tooth.
But let the frame of things disjoint, both the worlds suffer,
Ere we will eat our meal in fear, and sleep
20   In the affliction of these terrible dreams
That shake us nightly. Better be with the dead,
Whom we, to gain our peace, have sent to peace,

ACT THREE, Scene 2

LADY MACBETH *and a* SERVANT *enter.*

LADY MACBETH
Has Banquo left the court?

SERVANT
Yes, madam, but he'll be back tonight.

LADY MACBETH
Go tell the king I want to talk to him for a few minutes.

SERVANT
No problem, madam.

The SERVANT *exits.*

LADY MACBETH
If you get what you want and you're still not happy, you've spent everything and gained nothing. It's better to be the person who gets murdered than to be the killer and be tormented with anxiety.

MACBETH *enters.*

What's going on, my lord? Why are you keeping to yourself, with only your sad thoughts to keep you company? Those thoughts should have died when you killed the men you're thinking about. If you can't fix it, you shouldn't give it a second thought. What's done is done.

MACBETH
We have slashed the snake but not killed it. It will heal and be as good as new, and we'll be threatened by its fangs once again. But the universe can fall apart, and heaven and earth crumble, before I'll eat my meals in fear and spend my nights tossing and turning with these nightmares I've been having. I'd rather be dead than endure this endless mental torture and harrowing sleep deprivation. We killed those men and sent

Than on the torture of the mind to lie
In restless ecstasy. Duncan is in his grave.
25   After life's fitful fever he sleeps well.
Treason has done his worst; nor steel nor poison,
Malice domestic, foreign levy, nothing
Can touch him further.

LADY MACBETH
                              Come on, gentle my lord,
Sleek o'er your rugged looks. Be bright and jovial
30   Among your guests tonight.

MACBETH
                              So shall I, love,
And so, I pray, be you. Let your remembrance
Apply to Banquo; present him eminence,
Both with eye and tongue: unsafe the while that we
Must lave our honors in these flattering streams,
35   And make our faces vizards to our hearts,
Disguising what they are.

LADY MACBETH
                              You must leave this.

MACBETH
Oh, full of scorpions is my mind, dear wife!
Thou know'st that Banquo, and his Fleance, lives.

LADY MACBETH
But in them nature's copy's not eterne.

MACBETH
40   There's comfort yet; they are assailable.
Then be thou jocund. Ere the bat hath flown
His cloistered flight, ere to black Hecate's summons
The shard-borne beetle with his drowsy hums
Hath rung night's yawning peal, there shall be done
45   A deed of dreadful note.

LADY MACBETH
                              What's to be done?

them to rest in peace so that we could gain our own peace. Duncan lies in his grave, through with life's troubles, and he's sleeping well. We have already done the worst we can do to him with our treason. After that, nothing can hurt him further—not weapons, poison, rebellion, invasion, or anything else.

LADY MACBETH

Come on, relax, dear. Put on a happy face and look cheerful and agreeable for your guests tonight.

MACBETH

That's exactly what I'll do, my love, and I hope you'll do the same. Give Banquo your special attention. Talk to him and look at him in a way that will make him feel important. We're in a dangerous situation, where we have to flatter him and hide our true feelings.

LADY MACBETH

You have to stop talking like this.

MACBETH

Argh! I feel like my mind is full of scorpions, my dear wife. You know that Banquo and his son Fleance are still alive.

LADY MACBETH

But they can't live forever.

MACBETH

That's comforting. They can be killed, it's true. So be cheerful. Before the bat flies through the castle, and before the dung beetle makes his little humming noise to tell us it's nighttime, a dreadful deed will be done.

LADY MACBETH

What are you going to do?

MACBETH
          Be innocent of the knowledge, dearest chuck,
          Till thou applaud the deed. Come, seeling night,
          Scarf up the tender eye of pitiful day
          And with thy bloody and invisible hand
50   Cancel and tear to pieces that great bond
          Which keeps me pale. Light thickens, and the crow
          Makes wing to th' rooky wood.
          Good things of day begin to droop and drowse;
          Whiles night's black agents to their preys do rouse.
55   Thou marvel'st at my words: but hold thee still.
          Things bad begun make strong themselves by ill.
          So, prithee, go with me.
                                                        Exeunt

MACBETH

It's better you don't know about it until after it's done, when you can applaud it. *(to the night)* Come, night, and blindfold the kindhearted day. Use your bloody and invisible hand to tear up Banquo's lease on life, which keeps me in fear. *(to himself)* The sky's getting dark, and the crow is returning home to the woods. The gentle creatures of the day are falling asleep, while night's predators are waking up to look for their prey. *(to* LADY MACBETH*)* You seem surprised at my words, but don't question me yet. Bad deeds force you to commit more bad deeds. So please, come with me.

They exit.

ACT THREE, Scene 3

Enter three MURDERERS

FIRST MURDERER
But who did bid thee join with us?

THIRD MURDERER
Macbeth.

SECOND MURDERER
He needs not our mistrust, since he delivers
Our offices and what we have to do
5   To the direction just.

FIRST MURDERER
           Then stand with us.
The west yet glimmers with some streaks of day.
Now spurs the lated traveler apace
To gain the timely inn, and near approaches
The subject of our watch.

THIRD MURDERER
           Hark, I hear horses.

BANQUO
10   *(within)* Give us a light there, ho!

SECOND MURDERER
           Then 'tis he: the rest
That are within the note of expectation
Already are i' th' court.

FIRST MURDERER
           His horses go about.

THIRD MURDERER
Almost a mile; but he does usually—
So all men do—from hence to the palace gate
15   Make it their walk.

Enter BANQUO *and* FLEANCE *with a torch*

ACT THREE, Scene 3

The two MURDERERS *enter with a third* MURDERER.

FIRST MURDERER
But who told you to come here and join us?

THIRD MURDERER
Macbeth.

SECOND MURDERER
We can trust this guy. He was given exactly the same orders we were.

FIRST MURDERER
Then stay with us. There's still a bit of daylight in the sky. Now all the late travellers are hurrying to reach their inns. Banquo is almost here.

THIRD MURDERER
Listen! I hear horses.

BANQUO
(from offstage) Hey, give us some light here!

SECOND MURDERER
That must be him. The rest of the king's guests are already inside.

FIRST MURDERER
You can hear his horses moving around as the servants take them to the stables.

THIRD MURDERER
It's almost a mile to the palace gate, but Banquo, like everybody else, usually walks from here to the palace.

BANQUO *and* FLEANCE *enter with a torch.*

SECOND MURDERER
A light, a light!

THIRD MURDERER
'Tis he.

FIRST MURDERER
Stand to 't.

BANQUO
It will be rain tonight.

FIRST MURDERER
Let it come down.

The MURDERERS *attack* BANQUO

BANQUO
O treachery! Fly, good Fleance, fly, fly, fly!
Thou may 'st revenge —O slave!

BANQUO *dies. Exit* FLEANCE

THIRD MURDERER
20   Who did strike out the light?

FIRST MURDERER
Was 't not the way?

THIRD MURDERER
There's but one down. The son is fled.

SECOND MURDERER
We have lost best half of our affair.

FIRST MURDERER
Well, let's away and say how much is done.

Exeunt

SECOND MURDERER
> Here comes a light! Here comes a light!

THIRD MURDERER
> That's him.

FIRST MURDERER
> Prepare yourselves.

BANQUO
> It will rain tonight.

FIRST MURDERER
> Then let the rain come down.

The MURDERERS *attack* BANQUO.

BANQUO
> Oh, this is treachery! Get out of here, good Fleance,
> run, run, run! Someday you can get revenge.—Oh,
> you bastard!

> > BANQUO *dies.* FLEANCE *escapes.*

THIRD MURDERER
> Who put out the light?

FIRST MURDERER
> Wasn't that the best thing to do?

THIRD MURDERER
> There's only one body here. The son ran away.

SECOND MURDERER
> We failed in half of our mission.

FIRST MURDERER
> Well, let's get out of here and tell Macbeth what we
> did accomplish.

> > *They exit.*

—∽—

ACT THREE, Scene 4

Banquet prepared. Enter MACBETH, LADY MACBETH, ROSS, LENNOX, LORDS, *and attendants.*

MACBETH
You know your own degrees; sit down. At first
And last, the hearty welcome.

The LORDS *sit*

LORDS
Thanks to your majesty.

MACBETH
Ourself will mingle with society
And play the humble host.
5 Our hostess keeps her state, but in best time
We will require her welcome.

LADY MACBETH
Pronounce it for me, sir, to all our friends,
For my heart speaks they are welcome.

Enter FIRST MURDERER *at the door*

MACBETH
See, they encounter thee with their hearts' thanks.
10 Both sides are even. Here I'll sit i' th' midst.
Be large in mirth. Anon we'll drink a measure
The table round.
(aside to FIRST MURDERER*)* There's blood upon thy face.

FIRST MURDERER
'Tis Banquo's then.

MACBETH
'Tis better thee without than he within.
15 Is he dispatched?

ACT THREE, Scene 4

The stage is set for a banquet. MACBETH *enters with* LADY
MACBETH, ROSS, LENNOX, LORDS, *and their attendants.*

MACBETH
You know your own ranks, so you know where to sit.
Sit down. From the highest to the lowest of you, I bid
you a hearty welcome.

The LORDS *sit down.*

LORDS
Thanks to your majesty.

MACBETH
I will walk around and mingle with all of you, playing
the humble host. My wife will stay in her royal chair,
but at the appropriate time I will have her welcome
you all.

LADY MACBETH
Say welcome to all of our friends for me, sir, for in my
heart they are all welcome.

The FIRST MURDERER *appears at the door.*

MACBETH
And they respond to you with their hearts as well. The
table is full on both sides. I will sit here in the middle.
Be free and happy. Soon we will toast around the table.
(approaching the door and speaking to the MURDERER*)*
There's blood on your face.

FIRST MURDERER
Then it must be Banquo's.

MACBETH
I'd rather see his blood splattered on your face than
flowing through his veins. Did you finish him off?

FIRST MURDERER
My lord, his throat is cut. That I did for him.

MACBETH
Thou art the best o' th' cutthroats:
Yet he's good that did the like for Fleance.
If thou didst it, thou art the nonpareil.

FIRST MURDERER
20   Most royal sir, Fleance is 'scaped.

MACBETH
Then comes my fit again. I had else been perfect,
Whole as the marble, founded as the rock,
As broad and general as the casing air.
But now I am cabined, cribbed, confined, bound in
25   To saucy doubts and fears.—But Banquo's safe?

FIRST MURDERER
Ay, my good lord. Safe in a ditch he bides,
With twenty trenchèd gashes on his head,
The least a death to nature.

MACBETH
Thanks for that.
There the grown serpent lies. The worm that's fled
30   Hath nature that in time will venom breed;
No teeth for th' present. Get thee gone. Tomorrow
We'll hear ourselves again.

Exit **FIRST MURDERER**

LADY MACBETH
My royal lord,
You do not give the cheer. The feast is sold
That is not often vouched, while 'tis a-making,
35   'Tis given with welcome. To feed were best at home;
From thence, the sauce to meat is ceremony;
Meeting were bare without it.

FIRST MURDERER
My lord, his throat is cut. I did that to him.

MACBETH
You are the best of the cutthroats. But whoever did the same to Fleance must also be good. If you cut both their throats, then you are the absolute best.

FIRST MURDERER
Most royal sir, Fleance has escaped.

MACBETH
Now I'm scared again. Otherwise I would have been perfect, as solid as a piece of marble, as firm as a rock, as free as the air itself. But now I'm all tangled up with doubts and fears. But Banquo's been taken care of?

FIRST MURDERER
Yes, my good lord. He's lying dead in a ditch, with twenty deep gashes in his head, any one of which would have been enough to kill him.

MACBETH
Thanks for that. The adult snake lies in the ditch. The young snake that escaped will in time become poisonous and threatening, but for now he has no fangs. Get out of here. I'll talk to you again tomorrow.

The **FIRST MURDERER** *exits.*

LADY MACBETH
My royal lord, you're not entertaining the guests. If you don't make your guests know they're welcome, they'll feel like they're paying for their meal. When you just want to eat, it's better to do that at home. When you're eating out with people, you need to have a little more ceremony. Otherwise dinner parties would be boring.

MACBETH
                                    Sweet remembrancer!
Now, good digestion wait on appetite,
And health on both!

LENNOX
                          May 't please your highness sit.

Enter the GHOST OF BANQUO, *and sits in* MACBETH'S *place*

MACBETH
40   Here had we now our country's honor roofed,
Were the graced person of our Banquo present,
Who may I rather challenge for unkindness
Than pity for mischance.

ROSS
                                    His absence, sir,
Lays blame upon his promise. Please 't your highness
45   To grace us with your royal company?

MACBETH
The table's full.

LENNOX
                          Here is a place reserved, sir.

MACBETH
Where?

LENNOX
Here, my good lord. What is 't that moves your highness?

MACBETH
Which of you have done this?

LORDS
                                    What, my good lord?

MACBETH
50   *(to* GHOST*)* Thou canst not say I did it. Never shake
Thy gory locks at me.

MACBETH

It's nice of you to remind me. *(raising a glass to toast his guests)* Since good digestion requires a good appetite, and good health requires both of those, here's to good appetites, good digestion, and good health!

LENNOX

Why don't you have a seat, your highness?

The **GHOST OF BANQUO** *enters and sits in* **MACBETH**'*s place.*

MACBETH

We would have all the nobility of Scotland gathered under one roof, if only Banquo were here. I hope it turns out that he's late out of rudeness, and not because something bad has happened to him.

ROSS

His absence means he's broken his promise, sir. If it pleases you, your highness, why don't you sit with us and grace us with your royal company?

MACBETH

The table's full.

LENNOX

Here's an empty seat, sir.

MACBETH

Where?

LENNOX

(pointing to where the **GHOST** *sits)* Here, my good lord. What's wrong, your highness?

MACBETH

(seeing the **GHOST***)* Which one of you did this?

LORDS

What, my good lord?

MACBETH

(to the **GHOST***)* You can't say I did it. Don't shake your bloody head at me.

ROSS
Gentlemen, rise. His highness is not well.

LADY MACBETH
Sit, worthy friends. My lord is often thus
And hath been from his youth. Pray you, keep seat.
55 The fit is momentary; upon a thought
He will again be well. If much you note him,
You shall offend him and extend his passion.
Feed and regard him not. *(aside to* MACBETH*)* Are you a man?

MACBETH
Ay, and a bold one, that dare look on that
60 Which might appall the devil.

LADY MACBETH
O proper stuff!
This is the very painting of your fear.
This is the air-drawn dagger which you said
Led you to Duncan. Oh, these flaws and starts,
Impostors to true fear, would well become
65 A woman's story at a winter's fire,
Authorized by her grandam. Shame itself!
Why do you make such faces? When all's done,
You look but on a stool.

MACBETH
Prithee, see there! Behold! Look! Lo! How say you?
70 Why, what care I? If thou canst nod, speak too.
If charnel houses and our graves must send
Those that we bury back, our monuments
Shall be the maws of kites.

Exit GHOST

LADY MACBETH
What, quite unmanned in folly?

ROSS

Gentlemen, stand up. His highness is not well.

LADY MACBETH

Sit down, worthy friends. My husband is often like this, and he has been since he was a child. Please stay seated. This is just a brief fit. In a moment he'll be well again. If you pay too much attention to him you'll make him angry, and that will make his convulsions go on longer. Eat your dinner and pay no attention to him. *(speaking so that only* MACBETH *can hear)* Are you a man?

MACBETH

Yes, and a brave one, who dares to look at something that would frighten the devil.

LADY MACBETH

Oh, that's nonsense! This is just another one of the hallucinations you always get when you're afraid. This is like that floating dagger you said was leading you toward Duncan. These outbursts of yours don't even look like real fear. They're more like how you would act if you were a woman telling a scary story by the fireside in front of her grandmother. Shame on you! Why are you making these faces? When the vision passes, you'll see that you're just looking at a stool.

MACBETH

Please, just look over there. Look! Look! See! *(to the* GHOST*)* What do you have to say? What do I care? If you can nod, then speak too. If the dead are going to return from their graves, then there's nothing to stop the birds from eating the bodies. So there's no point in our burying people.

The GHOST *vanishes.*

LADY MACBETH

What, has your foolishness paralyzed you completely?

MACBETH
If I stand here, I saw him.

LADY MACBETH
Fie, for shame!

MACBETH
75 Blood hath been shed ere now, i' th' olden time,
Ere humane statute purged the gentle weal;
Ay, and since too, murders have been performed
Too terrible for the ear. The time has been
That, when the brains were out, the man would die,
80 And there an end. But now they rise again
With twenty mortal murders on their crowns
And push us from our stools. This is more strange
Than such a murder is.

LADY MACBETH
My worthy lord,
Your noble friends do lack you.

MACBETH
I do forget.
85 Do not muse at me, my most worthy friends.
I have a strange infirmity, which is nothing
To those that know me. Come, love and health to all.
Then I'll sit down. Give me some wine. Fill full.

Enter the GHOST OF BANQUO

I drink to the general joy o' th' whole table,
90 And to our dear friend Banquo, whom we miss;
Would he were here! To all and him we thirst,
And all to all.

LORDS
Our duties, and the pledge.

They drink

MACBETH
As sure as I'm standing here, I saw him.

LADY MACBETH
Nonsense!

MACBETH
In ancient times, before there were laws to make the land safe and peaceful, a lot of blood was spilled. Yes, and since then murders have been committed that are too awful to talk about. It used to be that when you knocked a man's brains out he would just die, and that would be it. But now they rise from the dead with twenty fatal head wounds and push us off our stools. This haunting business is even stranger than murder.

LADY MACBETH
My worthy lord, your noble friends miss your company.

MACBETH
I forgot about them. *(to the guests)* Don't be alarmed on my account, my most worthy friends. I have a strange disorder, which no longer shocks those who know me well. *(raising his glass to toast the company)* Come, let's drink a toast: love and health to you all. Now I'll sit down. Give me some wine. Fill up my cup.

The GHOST OF BANQUO *reappears in* MACBETH'S *seat.*

I drink to the happiness of everyone at the table, and to our dear friend Banquo, whom we miss. I wish he were here! Let's drink to everyone here, and to Banquo. Now, everybody, drink

LORDS
Hear, hear.

They drink.

MACBETH
(*seeing the* GHOST) Avaunt, and quit my sight! Let the earth
    hide thee.
Thy bones are marrowless, thy blood is cold.
95   Thou hast no speculation in those eyes
Which thou dost glare with!

LADY MACBETH
                    Think of this, good peers,
But as a thing of custom. 'Tis no other;
Only it spoils the pleasure of the time.

MACBETH
What man dare, I dare.
100   Approach thou like the rugged Russian bear,
The armed rhinoceros, or th' Hyrcan tiger;
Take any shape but that, and my firm nerves
Shall never tremble. Or be alive again,
And dare me to the desert with thy sword.
105   If trembling I inhabit then, protest me
The baby of a girl. Hence, horrible shadow!
Unreal mockery, hence!

Exit GHOST

              Why so, being gone,
I am a man again. Pray you sit still.

LADY MACBETH
You have displaced the mirth, broke the good meeting,
110   With most admired disorder.

MACBETH
                  Can such things be,
And overcome us like a summer's cloud,
Without our special wonder? You make me strange
Even to the disposition that I owe,
When now I think you can behold such sights,
115   And keep the natural ruby of your cheeks,
When mine is blanched with fear.

MACBETH

(to the GHOST*)* Go! And get out of my sight! Stay in your grave. There's no marrow in your bones, and your blood is cold. You're staring at me with eyes that have no power to see.

LADY MACBETH

Good friends, think of this as nothing more than a strange habit. It's nothing else. Too bad it's spoiling our pleasure tonight.

MACBETH

I am as brave as any other man. Come at me in the form of a rugged Russian bear, an armor-plated rhinoceros, or a tiger from Iran. Take any shape other than the one you have now and I will never tremble in fear. Or come back to life again and challenge me to a duel in some deserted place. If I tremble then, you can call me a little girl. Get out of here, you horrible ghost, you hallucination. Get out!

The GHOST *vanishes.*

Look, now that it's gone, I'm a man again. Please, remain seated.

LADY MACBETH

You have ruined our good cheer and disrupted the gathering by making a spectacle of yourself.

MACBETH

(to the guests) Can things like this happen so suddenly without making us all astonished? You make me feel like I don't know myself, when I see you looking at these terrible things and keeping a straight face, while my face has gone white with fear.

ROSS

What sights, my lord?

LADY MACBETH

I pray you, speak not. He grows worse and worse.
Question enrages him. At once, good night.
Stand not upon the order of your going,
120 But go at once.

LENNOX

Good night, and better health
Attend his majesty!

LADY MACBETH

A kind good night to all!

Exeunt all but MACBETH *and* LADY MACBETH

MACBETH

It will have blood, they say. Blood will have blood.
Stones have been known to move, and trees to speak.
Augurs and understood relations have
125 By magot pies and choughs and rooks brought forth
The secret'st man of blood.—What is the night?

LADY MACBETH

Almost at odds with morning, which is which.

MACBETH

How say'st thou that Macduff denies his person
At our great bidding?

LADY MACBETH

Did you send to him, sir?

MACBETH

130 I hear it by the way; but I will send.
There's not a one of them but in his house
I keep a servant fee'd. I will tomorrow—
And betimes I will—to the weird sisters.
More shall they speak, for now I am bent to know,
135 By the worst means, the worst. For mine own good,
All causes shall give way. I am in blood

ROSS

> What things, my lord?

LADY MACBETH

> Please, don't speak to him. He's getting worse and worse. Talk makes him crazy. Everybody, please leave right now. Don't bother exiting in the order of your rank, but just leave right away.

LENNOX

> Good night. I hope the king recovers soon!

LADY MACBETH

> A kind good night to all!

Everyone leaves except MACBETH *and* LADY MACBETH.

MACBETH

> There's an old saying: the dead will have their revenge. Gravestones have been known to move, and trees to speak, to bring guilty men to justice. The craftiest murderers have been exposed by the mystical signs made by crows and magpies. How late at night is it?

LADY MACBETH

> It's almost morning. You can't tell whether it's day or night.

MACBETH

> What do you think about the fact that Macduff refuses to come to me when I command him?

LADY MACBETH

> Did you send for him, sir?

MACBETH

> I've heard about this indirectly, but I will send for him. In every one of the lords' households I have a servant paid to spy for me. Tomorrow, while it's still early, I will go see the witches. They will tell me more, because I'm determined to know the worst about what's going to happen. My own safety is the only important thing now. I have walked so far into this

Stepped in so far that, should I wade no more,
Returning were as tedious as go o'er.
Strange things I have in head, that will to hand,
140   Which must be acted ere they may be scanned.

LADY MACBETH
You lack the season of all natures, sleep.

MACBETH
Come, we'll to sleep. My strange and self-abuse
Is the initiate fear that wants hard use.
We are yet but young in deed.

Exeunt

river of blood that even if I stopped now, it would be as hard to go back to being good as it is to keep killing people. I have some schemes in my head that I'm planning to put into action. I have to do these things before I have a chance to think about them.

LADY MACBETH

You haven't slept.

MACBETH

Yes, let's go to sleep. My strange self-delusions just come from inexperience. We're still just beginners when it comes to crime.

They exit.

ACT THREE, Scene 5

Thunder. Enter the three WITCHES *meeting* HECATE

FIRST WITCH
Why, how now, Hecate! You look angerly.

HECATE
Have I not reason, beldams as you are?
Saucy and overbold, how did you dare
To trade and traffic with Macbeth
5 In riddles and affairs of death,
And I, the mistress of your charms,
The close contriver of all harms,
Was never called to bear my part,
Or show the glory of our art?
10 And, which is worse, all you have done
Hath been but for a wayward son,
Spiteful and wrathful, who, as others do,
Loves for his own ends, not for you.
But make amends now. Get you gone,
15 And at the pit of Acheron
Meet me i' th' morning. Thither he
Will come to know his destiny.
Your vessels and your spells provide,
Your charms and everything beside.
20 I am for the air. This night I'll spend
Unto a dismal and a fatal end.
Great business must be wrought ere noon.
Upon the corner of the moon
There hangs a vap'rous drop profound.
25 I'll catch it ere it come to ground.
And that distilled by magic sleights
Shall raise such artificial sprites
As by the strength of their illusion
Shall draw him on to his confusion.

ORIGINAL TEXT

ACT THREE, Scene 5

Thunder. The three WITCHES *enter, meeting* HECATE.

FIRST WITCH
What's wrong, Hecate? You look angry.

HECATE
Don't I have a reason to be angry, you disobedient hags? How dare you give Macbeth riddles and prophecies about his future without telling me? I am your boss and the source of your powers. I am the one who secretly decides what evil things happen, but you never called me to join in and show off my own powers. And what's worse, you've done all this for a man who behaves like a spoiled brat, angry and hateful. Like all spoiled sons, he chases after what he wants and doesn't care about you. But you can make it up to me. Go away now and in the morning meet me in the pit by the river in hell. Macbeth will go there to learn his destiny. You bring your cauldrons, your spells, your charms, and everything else. I'm about to fly away. I'll spend tonight working to make something horrible happen. I have a lot to do before noon. An important droplet is hanging from the corner of the moon. I'll catch it before it falls to the ground. When I work it over with magic spells, the drop will produce magical spirits that will trick Macbeth with illusions.

ACT THREE

30   He shall spurn fate, scorn death, and bear
      His hopes 'bove wisdom, grace, and fear.
      And you all know, security
      Is mortals' chiefest enemy.

      Music and a song within: 'Come away, come away,' &c

      Hark! I am called. My little spirit, see,
35   Sits in a foggy cloud and stays for me.
                                                    Exit

      FIRST WITCH
      Come, let's make haste; she'll soon be back again.
                                                    Exeunt

He will be fooled into thinking he is greater than fate, he will mock death, and he will think he is above wisdom, grace, and fear. As you all know, overconfidence is man's greatest enemy.

Music plays offstage, and voices sing a song with the words "Come away, come away."

Listen! I'm being called. Look, my little spirit is sitting in a foggy cloud waiting for me.

HECATE *exits.*

FIRST WITCH
Come on, let's hurry. She'll be back again soon.

They all exit.

ACT THREE, Scene 6

Enter LENNOX *and another* LORD

LENNOX
My former speeches have but hit your thoughts,
Which can interpret farther. Only I say
Things have been strangely borne. The gracious Duncan
Was pitied of Macbeth. Marry, he was dead.
5   And the right-valiant Banquo walked too late,
Whom, you may say, if 't please you, Fleance killed,
For Fleance fled. Men must not walk too late.
Who cannot want the thought how monstrous
It was for Malcolm and for Donalbain
10 To kill their gracious father? Damnèd fact!
How it did grieve Macbeth! Did he not straight
In pious rage the two delinquents tear
That were the slaves of drink and thralls of sleep?
Was not that nobly done? Ay, and wisely too,
15 For 'twould have angered any heart alive
To hear the men deny 't. So that, I say,
He has borne all things well. And I do think
That had he Duncan's sons under his key—
As, an 't please heaven, he shall not—they should find
20 What 'twere to kill a father. So should Fleance.
But, peace! For from broad words, and 'cause he failed
His presence at the tyrant's feast, I hear
Macduff lives in disgrace. Sir, can you tell
Where he bestows himself?

LORD
                                    The son of Duncan—
25 From whom this tyrant holds the due of birth—
Lives in the English court and is received
Of the most pious Edward with such grace
That the malevolence of fortune nothing
Takes from his high respect. Thither Macduff

ACT THREE, Scene 6

LENNOX *and another* LORD *enter.*

LENNOX

What I've already said shows you we think alike, so you can draw your own conclusions. All I'm saying is that strange things have been going on. Macbeth pitied Duncan—after Duncan was dead. And Banquo went out walking too late at night. If you like, we can say that Fleance must have killed him, because Fleance fled the scene of the crime. Clearly, men should not go out walking too late! And who can help thinking how monstrous it was for Malcolm and Donalbain to kill their gracious father? Such a heinous crime—how it saddened Macbeth! Wasn't it loyal of him to kill those two servants right away, while they were still drunk and asleep? That was the right thing to do, wasn't it? Yes, and it was the wise thing, too, because we all would have been outraged to hear those two deny their crime. Considering all this, I think Macbeth has handled things well. If he had Duncan's sons in prison—which I hope won't happen—they would find out how awful the punishment is for those who kill their fathers, and so would Fleance. But enough of that. I hear that Macduff is out of favor with the king because he speaks his mind too plainly, and because he failed to show up at Macbeth's feast. Can you tell me where he's hiding himself?

Lennox speaks sarcastically throughout this speech, making it clear that he thinks Macbeth is guilty of the murders.

LORD

Duncan's son Malcolm, whose birthright and throne Macbeth has stolen, lives in the English court. There, the saintly King Edward treats Malcolm so well that despite Malcolm's misfortunes, he's not deprived of respect. Macduff went there to ask King Edward for help. He wants Edward to help him form an alliance

30   Is gone to pray the holy king upon his aid
       To wake Northumberland and warlike Siward,
       That by the help of these—with Him above
       To ratify the work—we may again
       Give to our tables meat, sleep to our nights,
35   Free from our feasts and banquets bloody knives,
       Do faithful homage and receive free honors.
       All which we pine for now. And this report
       Hath so exasperated the king that he
       Prepares for some attempt of war.

LENNOX
40   Sent he to Macduff?

LORD
       He did, and with an absolute "Sir, not I,"
       The cloudy messenger turns me his back,
       And hums, as who should say "You'll rue the time
       That clogs me with this answer."

LENNOX
                                        And that well might
45   Advise him to a caution, t' hold what distance
       His wisdom can provide. Some holy angel
       Fly to the court of England and unfold
       His message ere he come, that a swift blessing
       May soon return to this our suffering country
50   Under a hand accursed!

LORD
       I'll send my prayers with him.

                                        Exeunt

with the people of Northumberland and their lord, Siward. Macduff hopes that with their help—and with the help of God above—he may once again put food on our tables, bring peace back to our nights, free our feasts and banquets from violent murders, allow us to pay proper homage to our king, and receive honors freely. Those are the things we pine for now. Macbeth has heard this news and he is so angry that he's preparing for war.

LENNOX

Did he tell Macduff to return to Scotland?

LORD

He did, but Macduff told the messenger, "No way." The messenger scowled and rudely turned his back on Macduff, as if to say, "You'll regret the day you gave me this answer."

LENNOX

That might well keep Macduff away from Scotland. Some holy angel should go to the court of England and give Macduff a message. He should return quickly to free our country, which is suffering under a tyrant!

LORD

I'll send my prayers with him.

They exit.

ACT FOUR

Scene 1

A cavern. In the middle, a boiling cauldron. Thunder.
Enter the three WITCHES.

FIRST WITCH
Thrice the brinded cat hath mewed.

SECOND WITCH
Thrice, and once the hedge-pig whined.

THIRD WITCH
Harpier cries, "'Tis time, 'tis time."

FIRST WITCH
Round about the cauldron go,
5   In the poisoned entrails throw.
Toad, that under cold stone
Days and nights has thirty-one
Sweltered venom sleeping got,
Boil thou first i' th' charmèd pot.

ALL
10   Double, double toil and trouble,
Fire burn, and cauldron bubble.

SECOND WITCH
Fillet of a fenny snake,
In the cauldron boil and bake.
Eye of newt and toe of frog,
15   Wool of bat and tongue of dog,
Adder's fork and blind-worm's sting,
Lizard's leg and owlet's wing,
For a charm of powerful trouble,
Like a hell-broth boil and bubble.

ALL
20   Double, double toil and trouble,
Fire burn and cauldron bubble.

ACT FOUR

Scene 1

A cavern. In the middle, a boiling cauldron. Thunder.
The three WITCHES *enter.*

FIRST WITCH
> The tawny cat has meowed three times.

SECOND WITCH
> Three times. And the hedgehog has whined once.

THIRD WITCH
> My spirit friend, Harpier, is yelling, "It's time, it's time!"

FIRST WITCH
> Dance around the cauldron and throw in the poisoned entrails. *(holding up a toad)* You'll go in first—a toad that sat under a cold rock for a month, oozing poison from its pores.

ALL
> Double, double toil and trouble,
> Fire burn, and cauldron bubble.

SECOND WITCH
> *(holding something up)* We'll boil you in the cauldron next—a slice of swamp snake. All the rest of you in too: a newt's eye, a frog's tongue, fur from a bat, a dog's tongue, the forked tongue of an adder, the stinger of a burrowing worm, a lizard's leg, an owl's wing. *(speaking to the ingredients)* Make a charm to cause powerful trouble, and boil and bubble like a broth of hell.

ALL
> Double, double toil and trouble,
> Fire burn and cauldron bubble.

THIRD WITCH
Scale of dragon, tooth of wolf,
Witches' mummy, maw and gulf
Of the ravined salt-sea shark,
25   Root of hemlock digged i' th' dark,
Liver of blaspheming Jew,
Gall of goat and slips of yew
Slivered in the moon's eclipse,
Nose of Turk and Tartar's lips,
30   Finger of birth-strangled babe
Ditch-delivered by a drab,
Make the gruel thick and slab.
Add thereto a tiger's chaudron,
For the ingredients of our cauldron.

ALL
35   Double, double toil and trouble,
Fire burn and cauldron bubble.

SECOND WITCH
Cool it with a baboon's blood,
Then the charm is firm and good.

Enter HECATE *and the other three* WITCHES

HECATE
Oh well done! I commend your pains,
40   And every one shall share i' th' gains.
And now about the cauldron sing,
Like elves and fairies in a ring,
Enchanting all that you put in.

Music and a song: "Black spirits," &c. HECATE *retires*

SECOND WITCH
By the pricking of my thumbs,
45   Something wicked this way comes.
Open, locks,
Whoever knocks.

THIRD WITCH

Here come some more ingredients: the scale of a dragon, a wolf's tooth, a witch's mummified flesh, the gullet and stomach of a ravenous shark, a root of hemlock that was dug up in the dark, a Jew's liver, a goat's bile, some twigs of yew that were broken off during a lunar eclipse, a Turk's nose, a Tartar's lips, the finger of a baby that was strangled as a prostitute gave birth to it in a ditch. *(to the ingredients)* Make this potion thick and gluey. *(to the other* witches*)* Now let's add a tiger's entrails to the mix.

ALL

Double, double toil and trouble,
Fire burn and cauldron bubble.

SECOND WITCH

We'll cool the mixture with baboon blood. After that the charm is finished.

hecate *enters with three other* witches.

HECATE

Well done! I admire your efforts, and all of you will share the rewards. Now come sing around the cauldron like a ring of elves and fairies, enchanting everything you put in.

Music plays and the six witches *sing a song called "Black Spirits."* hecate *leaves.*

SECOND WITCH

I can tell that something wicked is coming by the tingling in my thumbs. Doors, open up for whoever is knocking!

Enter MACBETH

MACBETH
How now, you secret, black, and midnight hags?
What is 't you do?

ALL
                              A deed without a name.

MACBETH
50   I conjure you by that which you profess—
Howe'er you come to know it—answer me.
Though you untie the winds and let them fight
Against the churches, though the yeasty waves
Confound and swallow navigation up,
Though bladed corn be lodged and trees blown down,
55   Though castles topple on their warders' heads,
Though palaces and pyramids do slope
Their heads to their foundations, though the treasure
Of nature's germens tumble all together,
60   Even till destruction sicken, answer me
To what I ask you.

FIRST WITCH
                              Speak.

SECOND WITCH
                                   Demand.

THIRD WITCH
                                        We'll answer.

FIRST WITCH
Say, if th' hadst rather hear it from our mouths,
Or from our masters'.

MACBETH
                              Call 'em. Let me see 'em.

FIRST WITCH
Pour in sow's blood, that hath eaten
65   Her nine farrow; grease that's sweaten
From the murderer's gibbet throw
Into the flame.

MACBETH *enters.*

MACBETH
What's going on here, you secret, evil, midnight hags? What are you doing?

ALL
Something there isn't a word for.

MACBETH
I don't know how you know the things you do, but I insist that you answer my questions. I command you in the name of whatever dark powers you serve. I don't care if you unleash violent winds that tear down churches, make the foamy waves overwhelm ships and send sailors to their deaths, flatten crops and trees, make castles fall down on their inhabitants' heads, make palaces and pyramids collapse, and mix up everything in nature. Tell me what I want to know.

FIRST WITCH
Speak.

SECOND WITCH
Demand.

THIRD WITCH
We'll answer.

FIRST WITCH
Would you rather hear these things from our mouths or from our master's?

MACBETH
Call them. Let me see them.

FIRST WITCH
Pour in the blood of a sow who has eaten her nine offspring. Take the sweat of a murderer on the gallows and throw it into the flame.

ACT FOUR

ALL
> Come, high or low;
> Thyself and office deftly show!

Thunder. FIRST APPARITION: *an armed head*

MACBETH
> Tell me, thou unknown power—

FIRST WITCH
> He knows thy thought.
70 Hear his speech but say thou nought.

FIRST APPARITION
> Macbeth! Macbeth! Macbeth! Beware Macduff.
> Beware the thane of Fife. Dismiss me. Enough.

Descends

MACBETH
> Whate'er thou art, for thy good caution, thanks.
> Thou hast harped my fear aright. But one word more—

FIRST WITCH
75 He will not be commanded. Here's another
> More potent than the first.

Thunder. SECOND APPARITION: *a bloody child*

SECOND APPARITION
> Macbeth! Macbeth! Macbeth!—

MACBETH
> Had I three ears, I'd hear thee.

SECOND APPARITION
> Be bloody, bold, and resolute. Laugh to scorn
80 The power of man, for none of woman born
> Shall harm Macbeth.
> *Descends*

ALL

Come, high or low spirits. Show yourself and what you do.

Thunder. The FIRST APPARITION *appears, looking like a head with an armored helmet.*

MACBETH

Tell me, you unknown power—

FIRST WITCH

He can read your thoughts. Listen, but don't speak.

FIRST APPARITION

Macbeth! Macbeth! Macbeth! Beware Macduff. Beware the thane of Fife. Let me go. Enough.

The FIRST APPARITION *descends.*

MACBETH

Whatever you are, thanks for your advice. You have guessed exactly what I feared. But one word more—

FIRST WITCH

He will not be commanded by you. Here's another, stronger than the first.

Thunder. The SECOND APPARITION *appears, looking like a bloody child.*

SECOND APPARITION

Macbeth! Macbeth! Macbeth!

MACBETH

If I had three ears I'd listen with all three.

SECOND APPARITION

Be violent, bold, and firm. Laugh at the power of other men, because nobody born from a woman will ever harm Macbeth.

The SECOND APPARITION *descends.*

MACBETH
Then live, Macduff. What need I fear of thee?
But yet I'll make assurance double sure,
And take a bond of fate. Thou shalt not live,
85   That I may tell pale-hearted fear it lies,
And sleep in spite of thunder.

Thunder. **THIRD APPARITION**: *a child crowned,*
with a tree in his hand

What is this
That rises like the issue of a king,
And wears upon his baby-brow the round
And top of sovereignty?

ALL
Listen but speak not to 't.

THIRD APPARITION
90   Be lion-mettled, proud, and take no care
Who chafes, who frets, or where conspirers are.
Macbeth shall never vanquished be until
Great Birnam Wood to high Dunsinane Hill
Shall come against him.

Descends

MACBETH
That will never be.
95   Who can impress the forest, bid the tree
Unfix his earthbound root? Sweet bodements! Good!
Rebellious dead, rise never till the wood
Of Birnam rise, and our high-placed Macbeth
Shall live the lease of nature, pay his breath
100 To time and mortal custom. Yet my heart
Throbs to know one thing. Tell me, if your art
Can tell so much: shall Banquo's issue ever
Reign in this kingdom?

MACBETH

Then I don't need to kill Macduff. I have no reason to fear him. But even so, I'll make doubly sure. I'll guarantee my own fate by having you killed, Macduff. That way I can conquer my own fear and sleep easy at night.

Thunder. The THIRD APPARITION *appears, in the form of a child with a crown on his head and a tree in his hand.*

What is this spirit that looks like the son of a king and wears a crown on his young head?

ALL

Listen but don't speak to it.

THIRD APPARITION

Be brave like the lion and proud. Don't even worry about who hates you, who resents you, and who conspires against you. Macbeth will never be defeated until Birnam Wood marches to fight you at Dunsinane Hill.

The THIRD APPARITION *descends.*

MACBETH

That will never happen. Who can command the forest and make the trees pull their roots out of the earth? These were sweet omens! Good! My murders will never come back to threaten me until the forest of Birnam gets up and moves, and I will be king for my entire natural life. But my heart is still throbbing to know one thing. Tell me, if your dark powers can see this far: will Banquo's sons ever reign in this kingdom?

ALL
Seek to know no more.

MACBETH
I will be satisfied. Deny me this,
105 And an eternal curse fall on you! Let me know.
Why sinks that cauldron? And what noise is this?

Hautboys

FIRST WITCH
Show.

SECOND WITCH
Show.

THIRD WITCH
Show.

ALL
110 Show his eyes and grieve his heart.
Come like shadows; so depart!

A show of eight kings, the last with a glass
in his hand, followed by BANQUO

MACBETH
Thou art too like the spirit of Banquo. Down!
Thy crown does sear mine eyeballs. And thy hair,
Thou other gold-bound brow, is like the first.
115 A third is like the former.—Filthy hags!
Why do you show me this? A fourth? Start, eyes!
What, will the line stretch out to th' crack of doom?
Another yet? A seventh? I'll see no more.
And yet the eighth appears, who bears a glass
120 Which shows me many more, and some I see
That twofold balls and treble scepters carry.
Horrible sight! Now I see 'tis true;
For the blood-boltered Banquo smiles upon me
And points at them for his.

ALL

Don't try to find out more.

MACBETH

I demand to be satisfied. If you refuse, let an eternal curse fall on you. Let me know. Why is that cauldron sinking? And what is that music?

Hautboys play music for a ceremonial procession.

FIRST WITCH

Show.

SECOND WITCH

Show.

THIRD WITCH

Show.

ALL

Show him and make him grieve. Come like shadows and depart in the same way!

Eight kings march across the stage, the last one with a mirror in his hand, followed by the GHOST OF BANQUO.

MACBETH

You look too much like the ghost of Banquo. Go away! *(to the first)* Your crown hurts my eyes. *(to the second)* Your blond hair, which looks like another crown underneath the one you're wearing, looks just like the first king's hair. Now I see a third king who looks just like the second. Filthy hags! Why are you showing me this? A fourth! My eyes are bulging out of their sockets! Will this line stretch on forever? Another one! And a seventh! I don't want to see any more. And yet an eighth appears, holding a mirror in which I see many more men. And some are carrying double balls and triple scepters, meaning they're kings of more than one country! Horrible sight! Now I see it is true, they are Banquo's descendants. Banquo, with his blood-clotted hair, is smiling at me and pointing to them as his.

Apparitions vanish

What, is this so?

FIRST WITCH
125   Ay, sir, all this is so. But why
Stands Macbeth thus amazedly?
Come, sisters, cheer we up his sprites,
And show the best of our delights.
I'll charm th' air to give a sound,
130   While you perform your antic round.
That this great king may kindly say,
Our duties did his welcome pay.

Music. The WITCHES *dance and then vanish*

MACBETH
Where are they? Gone? Let this pernicious hour
Stand aye accursèd in the calendar!
135   Come in, without there.

Enter LENNOX

LENNOX
What's your grace's will?

MACBETH
Saw you the weird sisters?

LENNOX
No, my lord.

MACBETH
Came they not by you?

LENNOX
No, indeed, my lord.

MACBETH
Infected be the air whereon they ride,
And damned all those that trust them! I did hear
140   The galloping of horse. Who was 't came by?

The spirits of the kings and the GHOST OF BANQUO *vanish.*

What? Is this true?

FIRST WITCH

Yes, this is true, but why do you stand there so dumb-founded? Come, sisters, let's cheer him up and show him our talents. I will charm the air to produce music while you all dance around like crazy, so this king will say we did our duty and entertained him.

Music plays. The WITCHES *dance and then vanish.*

MACBETH

Where are they? Gone? Let this evil hour be marked forever in the calendar as cursed. *(calls to someone off-stage)* You outside, come in!

LENNOX *enters.*

LENNOX

What does your grace want?

MACBETH

Did you see the weird sisters?

LENNOX

No, my lord.

MACBETH

Didn't they pass by you?

LENNOX

No, indeed, my lord.

MACBETH

The air on which they ride is infected. Damn all those who trust them! I heard the galloping of horses. Who was it that came here?

LENNOX
'Tis two or three, my lord, that bring you word
Macduff is fled to England.

MACBETH
Fled to England?

LENNOX
Ay, my good lord.

MACBETH
145   Time, thou anticipat'st my dread exploits.
The flighty purpose never is o'ertook
Unless the deed go with it. From this moment
The very firstlings of my heart shall be
The firstlings of my hand. And even now,
150   To crown my thoughts with acts, be it thought and done:
The castle of Macduff I will surprise,
Seize upon Fife, give to th' edge o' th' sword
His wife, his babes, and all unfortunate souls
That trace him in his line. No boasting like a fool.
155   This deed I'll do before this purpose cool.
But no more sights!—Where are these gentlemen?
Come, bring me where they are.

Exeunt

LENNOX

Two or three men, my lord, who brought the message that Macduff has fled to England.

MACBETH

Fled to England?

LENNOX

Yes, my good lord.

MACBETH

Time, you thwart my dreadful plans. Unless a person does something the second he thinks of it, he'll never get a chance to do it. From now on, as soon as I decide to do something I'm going to act immediately. In fact, I'll start following up my thoughts with actions right now. I'll raid Macduff's castle, seize the town of Fife, and kill his wife, his children, and anyone else unfortunate enough to stand in line for his inheritance. No more foolish talk. I will do this deed before I lose my sense of purpose. But no more spooky visions!— Where are the messengers? Come, bring me to them.

They exit.

ACT FOUR, Scene 2

Enter LADY MACDUFF, *her* SON, *and* ROSS

LADY MACDUFF
What had he done to make him fly the land?

ROSS
You must have patience, madam.

LADY MACDUFF
                                    He had none.
His flight was madness. When our actions do not,
Our fears do make us traitors.

ROSS
                                    You know not
5   Whether it was his wisdom or his fear.

LADY MACDUFF
Wisdom! To leave his wife, to leave his babes,
His mansion and his titles in a place
From whence himself does fly? He loves us not;
He wants the natural touch. For the poor wren,
10   The most diminutive of birds, will fight,
Her young ones in her nest, against the owl.
All is the fear and nothing is the love,
As little is the wisdom, where the flight
So runs against all reason.

ROSS
                                    My dearest coz,
15   I pray you school yourself. But for your husband,
He is noble, wise, judicious, and best knows
The fits o' th' season. I dare not speak much further;
But cruel are the times when we are traitors
And do not know ourselves; when we hold rumor
20   From what we fear, yet know not what we fear,
But float upon a wild and violent sea
Each way and none. I take my leave of you.

ACT FOUR, Scene 2

LADY MACDUFF, *her* SON, *and* ROSS *enter.*

LADY MACDUFF
What did he do that made him flee this land?

ROSS
You have to be patient, madam.

LADY MACDUFF
He had no patience. He was crazy to run away. Even if you're not a traitor, you're going to look like one if you run away.

ROSS
You don't know whether it was wisdom or fear that made him flee.

LADY MACDUFF
How could it be wisdom! To leave his wife, his children, his house, and his titles in a place so unsafe that he himself flees it! He doesn't love us. He lacks the natural instinct to protect his family. Even the fragile wren, the smallest of birds, will fight against the owl when it threatens her young ones in the nest. His running away has everything to do with fear and nothing to do with love. And since it's so unreasonable for him to run away, it has nothing to do with wisdom either.

ROSS
My dearest relative, I'm begging you, pull yourself together. As for your husband, he is noble, wise, and judicious, and he understands what the times require. It's not safe for me to say much more than this, but times are bad when people get denounced as traitors and don't even know why. In times like these, we believe frightening rumors but we don't even know what we're afraid of. It's like being tossed around on the ocean in every direction, and finally getting nowhere. I'll say good-bye now. It won't be long

Shall not be long but I'll be here again.
Things at the worst will cease, or else climb upward
25   To what they were before.—My pretty cousin,
Blessing upon you.

LADY MACDUFF
Fathered he is, and yet he's fatherless.

ROSS
I am so much a fool, should I stay longer
It would be my disgrace and your discomfort.
30   I take my leave at once.

Exit

LADY MACDUFF
                        Sirrah, your father's dead.
And what will you do now? How will you live?

SON
As birds do, Mother.

LADY MACDUFF
                What, with worms and flies?

SON
With what I get, I mean, and so do they.

LADY MACDUFF
Poor bird! Thou 'dst never fear the net nor lime,
35   The pitfall nor the gin.

SON
Why should I, mother? Poor birds they are not set for.
My father is not dead, for all your saying.

LADY MACDUFF
Yes, he is dead. How wilt thou do for a father?

SON
Nay, how will you do for a husband?

LADY MACDUFF
40   Why, I can buy me twenty at any market.

before I'm back. When things are at their worst they have to stop, or else improve to the way things were before. My young cousin, I put my blessing upon you.

LADY MACDUFF
He has a father, and yet he is fatherless.

ROSS
I have to go. If I stay longer, I'll embarrass you and disgrace myself by crying. I'm leaving now.

ROSS exits.

LADY MACDUFF
Young man, your father's dead. What are you going to do now? How are you going to live?

SON
I will live the way birds do, Mother.

LADY MACDUFF
What? Are you going to start eating worms and flies?

SON
I mean I will live on whatever I get, like birds do.

LADY MACDUFF
You'd be a pitiful bird. You wouldn't know enough to be afraid of traps.

SON
Why should I be afraid of them, Mother? If I'm a pitiful bird, like you say, hunters won't want me. No matter what you say, my father is not dead.

LADY MACDUFF
Yes, he is dead. What are you going to do for a father?

SON
Maybe you should ask, what will you do for a husband?

LADY MACDUFF
Oh, I can buy twenty husbands at any market.

SON
Then you'll buy 'em to sell again.

LADY MACDUFF
Thou speak'st with all thy wit; and yet, i' faith,
With wit enough for thee.

SON
Was my father a traitor, Mother?

45 **LADY MACDUFF**
Ay, that he was.

SON
What is a traitor?

LADY MACDUFF
Why, one that swears and lies.

SON
And be all traitors that do so?

LADY MACDUFF
Every one that does so is a traitor and must be hanged.

50 **SON**
And must they all be hanged that swear and lie?

LADY MACDUFF
Every one.

SON
Who must hang them?

LADY MACDUFF
Why, the honest men.

SON
Then the liars and swearers are fools, for there are liars and
55 swearers enough to beat the honest men and hang up them.

LADY MACDUFF
Now, God help thee, poor monkey! But how wilt thou do
for a father?

SON
If he were dead, you'd weep for him. If you would not, it
were a good sign that I should quickly have a new father.

60 **LADY MACDUFF**
Poor prattler, how thou talk'st!

SON

If so, you'd be buying them to sell again.

LADY MACDUFF

You talk like a child, but you're very smart anyway.

SON

Was my father a traitor, Mother?

LADY MACDUFF

Yes, he was.

SON

What is a traitor?

LADY MACDUFF

Someone who makes a promise and breaks it.

SON

And is everyone who swears and lies a traitor?

LADY MACDUFF

Everyone who does so is a traitor and should be hanged.

SON

And should everyone who makes promises and breaks them be hanged?

LADY MACDUFF

Everyone.

SON

Who should hang them?

LADY MACDUFF

The honest men.

SON

Then the liars are fools, for there are enough liars in the world to beat up the honest men and hang them.

LADY MACDUFF

(laughing) Heaven help you for saying that, boy! *(sad again)* But what will you do without a father?

SON

If he were dead, you'd be weeping for him. If you aren't weeping, it's a good sign that I'll soon have a new father.

LADY MACDUFF

Silly babbler, how you talk!

Enter a MESSENGER

MESSENGER
  Bless you, fair dame! I am not to you known,
  Though in your state of honor I am perfect.
  I doubt some danger does approach you nearly.
  If you will take a homely man's advice,
65 Be not found here. Hence with your little ones.
  To fright you thus methinks I am too savage;
  To do worse to you were fell cruelty,
  Which is too nigh your person. Heaven preserve you!
  I dare abide no longer.

                                             Exit

LADY MACDUFF
                          Whither should I fly?
70 I have done no harm. But I remember now
  I am in this earthly world, where to do harm
  Is often laudable, to do good sometime
  Accounted dangerous folly. Why then, alas,
  Do I put up that womanly defense,
75 To say I have done no harm?

Enter MURDERERS

                          What are these faces?
FIRST MURDERER
  Where is your husband?
LADY MACDUFF
  I hope, in no place so unsanctified
  Where such as thou mayst find him.
FIRST MURDERER
                          He's a traitor.
SON
  Thou liest, thou shag-haired villain!

A MESSENGER *enters.*

MESSENGER
Bless you, fair lady! You don't know me, but I know you're an important person. I'm afraid something dangerous is coming toward you. If you'll take a simple man's advice, don't be here when it arrives. Go away and take your children. I feel bad for scaring you like this, but it would be much worse for me to let you come to harm. And harm is getting close! Heaven keep you safe!

The MESSENGER *exits.*

LADY MACDUFF
Where should I go? I haven't done anything wrong. But I have to remember that I'm here on Earth, where doing evil is often praised, and doing good is sometimes a stupid and dangerous mistake. So then why should I offer this womanish defense that I'm innocent?

The MURDERERS *enter.*

Who are these men?

FIRST MURDERER
Where is your husband?

LADY MACDUFF
I hope he's not anywhere so disreputable that thugs like you can find him.

FIRST MURDERER
He's a traitor.

SON
You're lying, you shaggy-haired villain!

FIRST MURDERER
    (Stabbing him)   What, you egg?
80   Young fry of treachery!

SON
    He has killed me, mother.
    Run away, I pray you!

He dies. Exit LADY MACDUFF,
crying "Murder!" followed by MURDERERS

FIRST MURDERER
What's that, you runt? *(stabbing him)* Young son of a traitor!

SON
He has killed me, Mother. Run away, I beg you!

The SON *dies.* LADY MACDUFF *exits, crying "Murder!" The* MURDERERS *exit, following her.*

ACT FOUR, Scene 3

Enter MALCOLM *and* MACDUFF

MALCOLM
Let us seek out some desolate shade and there
Weep our sad bosoms empty.

MACDUFF
                                        Let us rather
Hold fast the mortal sword and, like good men,
Bestride our downfall'n birthdom. Each new morn
New widows howl, new orphans cry, new sorrows
Strike heaven on the face, that it resounds
As if it felt with Scotland and yelled out
Like syllable of dolor.

MALCOLM
                                  What I believe I'll wail;
What know believe, and what I can redress,
As I shall find the time to friend, I will.
What you have spoke, it may be so perchance.
This tyrant, whose sole name blisters our tongues,
Was once thought honest. You have loved him well.
He hath not touched you yet. I am young, but something
You may deserve of him through me, and wisdom
To offer up a weak, poor, innocent lamb
T' appease an angry god.

MACDUFF
I am not treacherous.

MALCOLM
But Macbeth is.
A good and virtuous nature may recoil
In an imperial charge. But I shall crave your pardon.
That which you are, my thoughts cannot transpose.
Angels are bright still, though the brightest fell.
Though all things foul would wear the brows of grace,
Yet grace must still look so.

5

10

15

20

25

ACT FOUR, Scene 3

MALCOLM *and* MACDUFF *enter.*

MALCOLM
Let's seek out some shady place where we can sit down alone and cry our hearts out.

MACDUFF
Instead of crying, let's keep hold of our swords and defend our fallen homeland like honorable men. Each day new widows howl, new orphans cry, and new sorrows slap heaven in the face, until it sounds like heaven itself feels Scotland's anguish and screams in pain.

MALCOLM
I will avenge whatever I believe is wrong. And I'll believe whatever I'm sure is true. And I'll put right whatever I can when the time comes. What you just said may perhaps be true. This tyrant, whose mere name is so awful it hurts us to say it, was once considered an honest man. You were one of his favorites. He hasn't done anything to harm you yet. I'm inexperienced, but maybe you're planning to win Macbeth's favor by betraying me to him. It would be smart to offer someone poor and innocent like me as a sacrificial lamb to satisfy an angry god like Macbeth.

MACDUFF
I am not treacherous.

MALCOLM
But Macbeth is. Even someone with a good and virtuous nature might give way to a royal command. But I beg your pardon. My fears can't actually make you evil. Angels are still bright even though Lucifer, the brightest angel, fell from heaven. Even though everything evil wants to look good, good still has to look good too.

MACDUFF
                                   I have lost my hopes.

MALCOLM
Perchance even there where I did find my doubts.
Why in that rawness left you wife and child,
Those precious motives, those strong knots of love,
Without leave-taking? I pray you,
30   Let not my jealousies be your dishonors,
But mine own safeties. You may be rightly just,
Whatever I shall think.

MACDUFF
                              Bleed, bleed, poor country!
Great tyranny, lay thou thy basis sure,
For goodness dare not check thee. Wear thou thy wrongs;
35   The title is affeered.—Fare thee well, lord.
I would not be the villain that thou think'st
For the whole space that's in the tyrant's grasp,
And the rich East to boot.

MALCOLM
                                 Be not offended.
I speak not as in absolute fear of you.
40   I think our country sinks beneath the yoke.
It weeps, it bleeds, and each new day a gash
Is added to her wounds. I think withal
There would be hands uplifted in my right;
And here from gracious England have I offer
45   Of goodly thousands. But, for all this,
When I shall tread upon the tyrant's head,
Or wear it on my sword, yet my poor country
Shall have more vices than it had before,
More suffer, and more sundry ways than ever,
50   By him that shall succeed.

MACDUFF
                              What should he be?

MACDUFF

I have lost my hope of convincing you to fight against Macbeth.

MALCOLM

Maybe you lost your hopes about me where I found my doubts about you. Why did you leave your wife and child vulnerable—the most precious things in your life, those strong bonds of love? How could you leave them behind? But I beg you, don't interpret my suspicions as slander against you. You must understand that I want to protect myself. You may really be honest, no matter what I think.

MACDUFF

Bleed, bleed, poor country! Great tyrant, go ahead and build yourself up, because good people are afraid to stand up to you. Enjoy everything you stole, because your title is safe! Farewell, lord. I wouldn't be the villain you think I am even if I were offered all of Macbeth's kingdom and the riches of the East too.

MALCOLM

Don't be offended. I don't completely distrust you. I do think Scotland is sinking under Macbeth's oppression. Our country weeps, it bleeds, and each day a fresh cut is added to her wounds. I also think there would be many people willing to fight for me. The English have promised me thousands of troops. But even so, when I have Macbeth's head under my foot, or stuck on the end of my sword, then my poor country will be plagued by worse evil than it was before. It will suffer worse and in more ways than ever under the reign of the king who follows Macbeth.

MACDUFF

Who are you talking about?

ACT FOUR

MALCOLM
It is myself I mean, in whom I know
All the particulars of vice so grafted
That, when they shall be opened, black Macbeth
Will seem as pure as snow, and the poor state
55   Esteem him as a lamb, being compared
With my confineless harms.

MACDUFF
                                    Not in the legions
Of horrid hell can come a devil more damned
In evils to top Macbeth.

MALCOLM
                    I grant him bloody,
Luxurious, avaricious, false, deceitful,
60   Sudden, malicious, smacking of every sin
That has a name. But there's no bottom, none,
In my voluptuousness. Your wives, your daughters,
Your matrons, and your maids could not fill up
The cistern of my lust, and my desire
65   All continent impediments would o'erbear
That did oppose my will. Better Macbeth
Than such an one to reign.

MACDUFF
                                    Boundless intemperance
In nature is a tyranny. It hath been
The untimely emptying of the happy throne
70   And fall of many kings. But fear not yet
To take upon you what is yours. You may
Convey your pleasures in a spacious plenty
And yet seem cold; the time you may so hoodwink.
We have willing dames enough. There cannot be
75   That vulture in you to devour so many
As will to greatness dedicate themselves,
Finding it so inclined.

MALCOLM

I'm talking about myself. I know I have so many vices that when people see all of them exposed, evil Macbeth will seem as pure as snow in comparison, and poor Scotland will call him a sweet lamb when they compare him to me and my infinite evils.

MACDUFF

Even in hell you couldn't find a devil worse than Macbeth.

MALCOLM

I admit that he's murderous, lecherous, greedy, lying, deceitful, violent, malicious, and guilty of every sin that has a name. But there is no end, absolutely none, to my sexual desires. Your wives, your daughters, your old women, and your young maids together could not satisfy my lust. My desire would overpower all restraints and anyone who stood in my way. It would be better for Macbeth to rule than someone like me.

MACDUFF

Endless greed and lust in a man's nature is a kind of tyranny. It has caused the downfall of many kings. But don't be afraid to take the crown that belongs to you. You can find a way to satisfy your desires in secret, while still appearing virtuous. You can deceive everyone. There are more than enough willing women around. Your lust can't possibly be so strong that you'd use up all the women willing to give themselves to the king once they find out he wants them.

MALCOLM
　　With this there grows
　　In my most ill-composed affection such
80　A stanchless avarice that, were I king,
　　I should cut off the nobles for their lands,
　　Desire his jewels and this other's house.
　　And my more-having would be as a sauce
　　To make me hunger more, that I should forge
85　Quarrels unjust against the good and loyal,
　　Destroying them for wealth.

MACDUFF
　　　　　　　　　　　　　This avarice
　　Sticks deeper, grows with more pernicious root
　　Than summer-seeming lust, and it hath been
　　The sword of our slain kings. Yet do not fear;
90　Scotland hath foisons to fill up your will,
　　Of your mere own. All these are portable,
　　With other graces weighed.

MALCOLM
　　But I have none. The king-becoming graces,
　　As justice, verity, temperance, stableness,
95　Bounty, perseverance, mercy, lowliness,
　　Devotion, patience, courage, fortitude,
　　I have no relish of them but abound
　　In the division of each several crime,
　　Acting it many ways. Nay, had I power, I should
100　Pour the sweet milk of concord into hell,
　　Uproar the universal peace, confound
　　All unity on earth.

MACDUFF
　　　　　　　　　　O Scotland, Scotland!

MALCOLM
　　If such a one be fit to govern, speak.
　　I am as I have spoken.

MALCOLM

Along with being full of lust, I'm also incredibly greedy. If I became king, I would steal the nobles' lands, taking jewels from one guy and houses from another. The more I had, the greedier I would grow, until I'd invent false quarrels with my good and loyal subjects, destroying them so I could get my hands on their wealth.

MACDUFF

The greed you're talking about is worse than lust because you won't outgrow it. Greed has been the downfall of many kings. But don't be afraid. Scotland has enough treasures to satisfy you out of your own royal coffers. These bad qualities are bearable when balanced against your good sides.

MALCOLM

But I don't have any good sides. I don't have a trace of the qualities a king needs, such as justice, truth, moderation, stability, generosity, perseverance, mercy, humility, devotion, patience, courage, and bravery. Instead, I overflow with every variation of all the different vices. No, if I had power I would take world peace and throw it down to hell.

MACDUFF

Oh Scotland, Scotland!

MALCOLM

If someone like me is fit to be king, let me know. I really am exactly as I have described myself to you.

MACDUFF
                              Fit to govern?
105 No, not to live.—O nation miserable,
     With an untitled tyrant bloody-sceptered,
     When shalt thou see thy wholesome days again,
     Since that the truest issue of thy throne
     By his own interdiction stands accursed,
110 And does blaspheme his breed?—Thy royal father
     Was a most sainted king. The queen that bore thee,
     Oftener upon her knees than on her feet,
     Died every day she lived. Fare thee well!
     These evils thou repeat'st upon thyself
115 Have banished me from Scotland.—O my breast,
     Thy hope ends here!

MALCOLM
                         Macduff, this noble passion,
     Child of integrity, hath from my soul
     Wiped the black scruples, reconciled my thoughts
     To thy good truth and honor. Devilish Macbeth
120 By many of these trains hath sought to win me
     Into his power, and modest wisdom plucks me
     From overcredulous haste. But God above
     Deal between thee and me, for even now
     I put myself to thy direction and
125 Unspeak mine own detraction, here abjure
     The taints and blames I laid upon myself,
     For strangers to my nature. I am yet
     Unknown to woman, never was forsworn,
     Scarcely have coveted what was mine own,
130 At no time broke my faith, would not betray
     The devil to his fellow, and delight
     No less in truth than life. My first false speaking
     Was this upon myself. What I am truly,
     Is thine and my poor country's to command.

MACDUFF

(*to* MALCOLM) Fit to be king? You're not fit to live!—Oh miserable nation, ruled by a usurping, murderous tyrant, when will you see peaceful days again? The man who has a legal right to the throne is, by his own admission, a cursed man and a disgrace to the royal family.—Your royal father Duncan was a virtuous king. Your mother spent more time on her knees in prayer than she did standing up, and she lived a life of absolute piety. Good-bye. The evils you have described inside yourself have driven me out of Scotland forever. Oh my heart, your hope is dead!

MALCOLM

Macduff, this passionate outburst, which proves your integrity, has removed my doubts about you and made me realize that you really are trustworthy and honorable. That devil Macbeth has tried many times to trick me and lure me into his power, and prudence prevents me from believing people too quickly. But with God as my witness, I will let myself be guided by you, and I take back my confession. I take back all the bad things I said about myself, because none of those flaws are really part of my character. I'm still a virgin. I have never told a lie. I barely care about what I already own, let alone feel jealous of another's possessions. I have never broken a promise. I wouldn't betray the devil himself. I love truth as much as I love life. The lies I told about my character are actually the first false words I have ever spoken. The person who I really am is ready to serve you and our poor country.

ACT FOUR

135   Whither indeed, before thy here-approach,
Old Siward, with ten thousand warlike men,
Already at a point, was setting forth.
Now we'll together, and the chance of goodness
Be like our warranted quarrel! Why are you silent?

MACDUFF
140   Such welcome and unwelcome things at once
'Tis hard to reconcile.

Enter a DOCTOR

MALCOLM
Well, more anon.—Comes the king forth, I pray you?

DOCTOR
Ay, sir; there are a crew of wretched souls
That stay his cure. Their malady convinces
145   The great assay of art, but at his touch—
Such sanctity hath heaven given his hand—
They presently amend.

MALCOLM
                    I thank you, doctor.

Exit DOCTOR

MACDUFF
What's the disease he means?

MALCOLM
                    'Tis called the evil.
A most miraculous work in this good king,
150   Which often since my here-remain in England
I have seen him do. How he solicits heaven,
Himself best knows, but strangely visited people,
All swoll'n and ulcerous, pitiful to the eye,
The mere despair of surgery, he cures,
155   Hanging a golden stamp about their necks,
Put on with holy prayers. And, 'tis spoken,

Indeed, before you arrived here, old Siward, with ten thousand soldiers already prepared for battle, was making his way here. Now we will fight Macbeth together, and may the chances of our success be as great as the justice of our cause! Why are you silent?

MACDUFF

It's hard to make sense of such different stories.

A DOCTOR *enters.*

MALCOLM

Well, we'll speak more soon. *(to the* DOCTOR*)* Is King Edward coming out?

DOCTOR

Yes, sir. A crowd of sick people is waiting for him to heal them. Their illness confounds the most advanced techniques of modern medicine, but when he touches them, they heal immediately because of the power granted to him by heaven.

MALCOLM

Thank you, doctor.

The DOCTOR *exits.*

MACDUFF

What disease is he talking about?

MALCOLM

It's called the evil. Edward's healing touch is a miracle that I have seen him perform many times during my stay in England. How he receives these gifts from heaven, only he can say. But he cures people with strange conditions—all swollen, plagued by ulcers, and pitiful to look at, patients who are beyond the help of surgery—by placing a gold coin around their necks and saying holy prayers over them.

To the succeeding royalty he leaves
The healing benediction. With this strange virtue,
He hath a heavenly gift of prophecy,
160   And sundry blessings hang about his throne,
That speak him full of grace.

Enter ROSS

MACDUFF
                                        See, who comes here?

MALCOLM
My countryman, but yet I know him not.

MACDUFF
My ever-gentle cousin, welcome hither.

MALCOLM
I know him now.—Good God, betimes remove
165   The means that makes us strangers!

ROSS
                                                Sir, amen.

MACDUFF
Stands Scotland where it did?

ROSS
                                        Alas, poor country!
Almost afraid to know itself. It cannot
Be called our mother, but our grave, where nothing,
But who knows nothing, is once seen to smile;
170   Where sighs and groans and shrieks that rend the air
Are made, not marked; where violent sorrow seems
A modern ecstasy. The dead man's knell
Is there scarce asked for who, and good men's lives
Expire before the flowers in their caps,
175   Dying or ere they sicken.

MACDUFF
                                        Oh, relation
Too nice and yet too true!

They say that he bequeaths this ability to heal to his royal descendants. Along with this strange power, he also has the gift of prophecy and various other abilities. All of these signs mark him as a man graced by God.

ROSS *enters.*

MACDUFF

Who's that coming over here?

MALCOLM

By his dress I can tell he's my countryman, but I don't recognize him.

MACDUFF

My noble kinsman, welcome.

MALCOLM

I recognize him now. May God alter the circumstances that keep us apart!

ROSS

Hello, sir.

MACDUFF

Is Scotland the same as when I left it?

ROSS

Alas, our poor country! It's too frightened to look at itself. Scotland is no longer the land where we were born; it's the land where we'll die. Where no one ever smiles except for the fool who knows nothing. Where sighs, groans, and shrieks rip through the air but no one notices. Where violent sorrow is a common emotion. When the funeral bells ring, people no longer ask who died. Good men die before the flowers in their caps wilt. They die before they even fall sick.

MACDUFF

Oh, your report is too poetic, but it sounds so true!

ACT FOUR

MALCOLM
What's the newest grief?

ROSS
That of an hour's age doth hiss the speaker.
Each minute teems a new one.

MACDUFF
How does my wife?

ROSS
Why, well.

MACDUFF
And all my children?

ROSS
Well too.

MACDUFF
180   The tyrant has not battered at their peace?

ROSS
No, they were well at peace when I did leave 'em.

MACDUFF
Be not a niggard of your speech. How goes 't?

ROSS
When I came hither to transport the tidings,
Which I have heavily borne, there ran a rumor
185   Of many worthy fellows that were out;
Which was to my belief witnessed the rather
For that I saw the tyrant's power afoot.
Now is the time of help. Your eye in Scotland
Would create soldiers, make our women fight,
190   To doff their dire distresses.

MALCOLM
Be 't their comfort
We are coming thither. Gracious England hath
Lent us good Siward and ten thousand men;
An older and a better soldier none
That Christendom gives out.

MALCOLM

What is the most recent news?

ROSS

Even news an hour old is old news. Every minute another awful thing happens.

MACDUFF

How is my wife?

ROSS

She's well.

MACDUFF

And all my children?

ROSS

They're well too.

MACDUFF

Macbeth hasn't attacked them?

Lady Macduff and the children are "well" and "at peace" in the sense that they're dead.

ROSS

They were at peace when I left them.

MACDUFF

Don't be stingy with your words. What's the news?

ROSS

While I was coming here to tell you my sad news, I heard rumors that many good men are arming themselves to rebel against Macbeth. When I saw Macbeth's army on the move, I knew the rumors must be true. Now is the time when we need your help. Your presence in Scotland would inspire people to fight. Even the women would fight to rid themselves of Macbeth's oppression.

MALCOLM

Let them be comforted—I'm returning to Scotland. Gracious King Edward has sent us noble Siward and ten thousand soldiers. There is no soldier more experienced or successful than Siward in the entire Christian world.

ACT FOUR

ROSS
Would I could answer
195   This comfort with the like. But I have words
That would be howled out in the desert air,
Where hearing should not latch them.

MACDUFF
What concern they?
The general cause, or is it a fee-grief
Due to some single breast?

ROSS
No mind that's honest
200   But in it shares some woe, though the main part
Pertains to you alone.

MACDUFF
If it be mine,
Keep it not from me. Quickly let me have it.

ROSS
Let not your ears despise my tongue forever,
Which shall possess them with the heaviest sound
205   That ever yet they heard.

MACDUFF
Hum! I guess at it.

ROSS
Your castle is surprised, your wife and babes
Savagely slaughtered. To relate the manner,
Were, on the quarry of these murdered deer
To add the death of you.

MALCOLM
Merciful heaven!
210   What, man! Ne'er pull your hat upon your brows.
Give sorrow words. The grief that does not speak
Whispers the o'erfraught heart and bids it break.

MACDUFF
My children too?

ROSS
Wife, children, servants, all that could be found.

ROSS

I wish I could repay this happy news with good news of my own. But I have some news that should be howled in a barren desert where nobody can hear it.

MACDUFF

What is this news about? Does it affect all of us? Or just one of us?

ROSS

No decent man can keep from sharing in the sorrow, but my news affects you alone.

MACDUFF

If it's for me, don't keep it from me. Let me have it now.

ROSS

I hope you won't hate me forever after I say these things, because I will soon fill your ears with the most dreadful news you have ever heard.

MACDUFF

I think I can guess what you're about to say.

ROSS

Your castle was attacked. Your wife and children were savagely slaughtered. If I told you how they were killed, it would cause you so much pain that it would kill you too, and add your body to the pile of murdered corpses.

MALCOLM

Merciful heaven! *(to* MACDUFF*)* Come on, man, don't keep your grief hidden. Put your sorrow into words. The grief you keep inside you will whisper in your heart until it breaks.

MACDUFF

They killed my children too?

ROSS

They killed your wife, your children, your servants, anyone they could find.

MACDUFF
215 And I must be from thence!
My wife killed too?

ROSS
I have said.

MALCOLM
Be comforted.
Let's make us med'cines of our great revenge,
220 To cure this deadly grief.

MACDUFF
He has no children. All my pretty ones?
Did you say all? O hell-kite! All?
What, all my pretty chickens and their dam
At one fell swoop?

MALCOLM
225 Dispute it like a man.

MACDUFF
I shall do so,
But I must also feel it as a man.
I cannot but remember such things were
That were most precious to me. Did heaven look on,
230 And would not take their part? Sinful Macduff,
They were all struck for thee! Naught that I am,
Not for their own demerits, but for mine,
Fell slaughter on their souls. Heaven rest them now.

MALCOLM
Be this the whetstone of your sword. Let grief
235 Convert to anger. Blunt not the heart, enrage it.

MACDUFF
Oh, I could play the woman with mine eyes
And braggart with my tongue! But, gentle heavens,
Cut short all intermission. Front to front
Bring thou this fiend of Scotland and myself.
240 Within my sword's length set him; if he 'scape,
Heaven forgive him too.

MACDUFF

And I had to be away! My wife was killed too?

ROSS

I said she was.

MALCOLM

Take comfort. Let's cure this awful grief by taking revenge on Macbeth.

MACDUFF

He doesn't have children. All my pretty little children? Did you say all? Oh, that bird from hell! All of them? What, all my children and their mother dead in one fell swoop?

MALCOLM

Fight it like a man.

MACDUFF

I will. But I also have to feel it like a man. I can't help remembering the things that were most precious to me. Did heaven watch the slaughter and not send down any help? Sinful Macduff, they were killed because of you! As wicked as I am, they were slaughtered because of me, not because of anything they did. May God give their souls rest.

MALCOLM

Let this anger sharpen your sword. Transform your grief into anger. Don't block the feelings in your heart; let them loose as rage.

MACDUFF

I could go on weeping like a woman and bragging about how I will avenge them! But gentle heavens, don't keep me waiting. Bring me face to face with Macbeth, that devil of Scotland. Put him within the reach of my sword, and if he escapes, may heaven forgive him as well!

ACT FOUR

MALCOLM
                                        This tune goes manly.
Come, go we to the king. Our power is ready;
Our lack is nothing but our leave. Macbeth
Is ripe for shaking, and the powers above
245   Put on their instruments. Receive what cheer you may.
The night is long that never finds the day.
                                            Exeunt

MALCOLM
Now you sound like a man. Come on, let's go see King Edward. The army is ready. All we have to do now is say goodbye to the king. Macbeth is ripe for the picking. We'll be acting as God's agents. Cheer up as much as you can. A new day will come at last.

They exit.

ACT FIVE

Scene 1

Enter a DOCTOR *of physic and a waiting-*GENTLEWOMAN

DOCTOR
I have two nights watched with you but can perceive no
truth in your report. When was it she last walked?

GENTLEWOMAN
Since his majesty went into the field, I have seen her rise
from her bed, throw her nightgown upon her, unlock her
5   closet, take forth paper, fold it, write upon 't, read it,
afterwards seal it, and again return to bed; yet all this while
in a most fast sleep.

DOCTOR
A great perturbation in nature, to receive at once the benefit
of sleep, and do the effects of watching. In this slumbery
10   agitation, besides her walking and other actual
performances, what, at any time, have you heard her say?

GENTLEWOMAN
That, sir, which I will not report after her.

DOCTOR
You may to me, and 'tis most meet you should.

GENTLEWOMAN
Neither to you nor any one, having no witness to confirm
15   my speech.

Enter LADY MACBETH *with a taper*

Lo you, here she comes. This is her very guise; and, upon
my life, fast asleep. Observe her, stand close.

DOCTOR
How came she by that light?

ACT FIVE

Scene 1

The waiting-gentlewoman is an upperclass woman whose job is to wait on the queen.

A DOCTOR *and a waiting-*GENTLEWOMAN *enter.*

DOCTOR I've stayed up with you for two nights now, and I haven't seen any evidence of what you were talking about. When was the last time you saw her sleepwalking?

GENTLEWOMAN
Since Macbeth went to war, I have seen her rise from her bed, put on her nightgown, unlock her closet, take out some paper, fold it, write on it, read it, seal it up, and then return to bed, remaining asleep the entire time.

DOCTOR
It's unnatural to be asleep and act as if you're awake. When she is like this, besides walking and performing various activities, have you heard her say anything?

GENTLEWOMAN
She says something, sir, but I will not repeat it to you.

DOCTOR
You can tell me. You really should.

GENTLEWOMAN
I will not confess it to you nor to anyone else, because there was no one else to witness her speech.

LADY MACBETH *enters, holding a candle.*

Look, here she comes! This is exactly how she always looks, and—I swear it—she is fast asleep. Watch her. Keep hidden.

DOCTOR
How did she get that candle?

GENTLEWOMAN
Why, it stood by her. She has light by her continually. 'Tis
20   her command.

DOCTOR
You see her eyes are open.

GENTLEWOMAN
Ay, but their sense is shut.

DOCTOR
What is it she does now? Look, how she rubs her hands.

GENTLEWOMAN
It is an accustomed action with her to seem thus washing
25   her hands. I have known her continue in this a quarter of an
hour.

LADY MACBETH
Yet here's a spot.

DOCTOR
Hark! She speaks. I will set down what comes from her, to
satisfy my remembrance the more strongly.

LADY MACBETH
30   Out, damned spot! Out, I say!—One, two. Why, then, 'tis
time to do 't. Hell is murky!—Fie, my lord, fie! A soldier,
and afeard? What need we fear who knows it, when none
can call our power to account?—Yet who would have
thought the old man to have had so much blood in him.

DOCTOR
35   Do you mark that?

LADY MACBETH
The thane of Fife had a wife. Where is she now?—What,
will these hands ne'er be clean?—No more o' that, my lord,
no more o' that. You mar all with this starting.

DOCTOR
Go to, go to. You have known what you should not.

GENTLEWOMAN

It stands by her bedside. She always has to have a light next to her. Those are her orders.

DOCTOR

You see, her eyes are open.

GENTLEWOMAN

Yes, but they don't see anything.

DOCTOR

What's she doing now? Look how she rubs her hands.

GENTLEWOMAN

She often does that. She looks like she's washing her hands. I've seen her do that before for as long as fifteen minutes.

LADY MACBETH

There's still a spot here.

DOCTOR

Listen! She's talking. I'll write down what she says, so I'll remember it better.

LADY MACBETH

(rubbing her hands) Come out, damned spot! Out, I command you! One, two. OK, it's time to do it now.— Hell is murky!—Nonsense, my lord, nonsense! You are a soldier, and yet you are afraid? Why should we be scared, when no one can lay the guilt upon us?—But who would have thought the old man would have had so much blood in him?

DOCTOR

Did you hear that?

LADY MACBETH

The thane of Fife had a wife. Where is she now?— What, will my hands never be clean?—No more of that, my lord, no more of that. You'll ruin everything by acting startled like this.

DOCTOR

Now look what you've done. You've heard something you shouldn't have.

ACT FIVE

GENTLEWOMAN
40   She has spoke what she should not, I am sure of that.
        Heaven knows what she has known.

LADY MACBETH
        Here's the smell of the blood still. All the perfumes of
        Arabia will not sweeten this little hand. Oh, Oh, Oh!

DOCTOR
        What a sigh is there! The heart is sorely charged.

GENTLEWOMAN
45   I would not have such a heart in my bosom for the dignity
        of the whole body.

DOCTOR
        Well, well, well.

GENTLEWOMAN
        Pray God it be, sir.

DOCTOR
        This disease is beyond my practice. Yet I have known those
50   which have walked in their sleep who have died holily in
        their beds.

LADY MACBETH
        Wash your hands. Put on your nightgown. Look not so
        pale.—I tell you yet again, Banquo's buried; he cannot
        come out on 's grave.

DOCTOR
55   Even so?

LADY MACBETH
        To bed, to bed. There's knocking at the gate. Come, come,
        come, come. Give me your hand. What's done cannot be
        undone.—To bed, to bed, to bed!

                                                           Exit

DOCTOR
        Will she go now to bed?

GENTLEWOMAN
> She said something she shouldn't have said, I'm sure of that. Heaven knows what secrets she's keeping.

LADY MACBETH
> I still have the smell of blood on my hand. All the perfumes of Arabia couldn't make my little hand smell better. Oh, oh, oh!

DOCTOR
> What a heavy sigh! Her heart is carrying a heavy weight.

GENTLEWOMAN
> I wouldn't want a heart like hers even if you made me queen.

DOCTOR
> Well, well, well.

GENTLEWOMAN
> I hope what she's saying is well, sir!

DOCTOR
> This disease is beyond my medical skills. But I have known people who sleepwalked and weren't guilty of anything.

LADY MACBETH
> Wash your hands. Put on your nightgown. Don't look so frightened. I tell you again, Banquo is buried. He cannot come out of his grave.

DOCTOR
> Is this true?

LADY MACBETH
> To bed, to bed! There's a knocking at the gate. Come, come, come, come, give me your hand. What's done cannot be undone. To bed, to bed, to bed!

> **LADY MACBETH** *exits.*

DOCTOR
> Will she go to bed now?

GENTLEWOMAN
60   Directly.

DOCTOR
Foul whisp'rings are abroad. Unnatural deeds
Do breed unnatural troubles. Infected minds
To their deaf pillows will discharge their secrets.
More needs she the divine than the physician.
65   God, God forgive us all! Look after her,
Remove from her the means of all annoyance,
And still keep eyes upon her. So, good night.
My mind she has mated, and amazed my sight.
I think, but dare not speak.

GENTLEWOMAN
Good night, good doctor.

Exeunt

GENTLEWOMAN
Yes, right away.

DOCTOR
Evil rumors are going around. Unnatural acts will cause supernatural things to happen. People with guilty and deranged minds will confess their secrets to their pillows as they sleep. This woman needs a priest more than a doctor. God forgive us all! *(to the waiting-* **GENTLEWOMAN***)* Look after her. Remove anything she might hurt herself with. Watch her constantly. And now, good-night. She has bewildered my mind and amazed my eyes. I have an opinion, but I don't dare to say it out loud.

Sleepwalking and sleeptalking were considered super-natural events in Shakespeare's time.

GENTLEWOMAN
Good night, good doctor.

They exit.

ACT FIVE, Scene 2

Drum and colors. Enter MENTEITH, CAITHNESS, ANGUS, LENNOX, *and soldiers*

MENTEITH
The English power is near, led on by Malcolm,
His uncle Siward and the good Macduff.
Revenges burn in them, for their dear causes
Would to the bleeding and the grim alarm
5   Excite the mortified man.

ANGUS
                              Near Birnam Wood
Shall we well meet them; that way are they coming.

CAITHNESS
Who knows if Donalbain be with his brother?

LENNOX
For certain, sir, he is not. I have a file
Of all the gentry. There is Siward's son,
10   And many unrough youths that even now
Protest their first of manhood.

MENTEITH
                              What does the tyrant?

CAITHNESS
Great Dunsinane he strongly fortifies.
Some say he's mad, others that lesser hate him
Do call it valiant fury. But, for certain,
15   He cannot buckle his distempered cause
Within the belt of rule.

ANGUS
                              Now does he feel
His secret murders sticking on his hands.
Now minutely revolts upbraid his faith-breach.
Those he commands move only in command,
20   Nothing in love. Now does he feel his title
Hang loose about him, like a giant's robe
Upon a dwarfish thief.

ACT FIVE, Scene 2

MENTEITH, CAITHNESS, ANGUS, LENNOX, *and soldiers*
enter with a drummer and flag.

MENTEITH

The English army is near, led by Malcolm, his uncle
Siward, and the good Macduff. They burn for
revenge. The wrongs they have suffered would make
dead men rise up and fight.

ANGUS

We'll meet them near Birnam Wood. They are coming
that way.

CAITHNESS

Does anyone know if Donalbain is with his brother?

LENNOX

He is definitely not there, sir. I have a list of all the
important men. Siward's son is there, as well as many
boys too young to have beards who will become men
by joining in this battle.

MENTEITH

What is the tyrant Macbeth doing?

CAITHNESS

He is fortifying his castle at Dunsinane with heavy
defenses. Some say he's insane. Those who hate him
less call it brave anger. One thing is certain: he's out of
control.

ANGUS

Now Macbeth feels the blood of his murdered enemies sticking to his hands. Now, rebel armies punish
him every minute for his treachery. The soldiers he
commands are only following orders. They don't fight
because they love Macbeth. Now he seems too small
to be a great king, like a dwarf trying to wear the
robes of a giant.

MENTEITH
                              Who then shall blame
His pestered senses to recoil and start,
When all that is within him does condemn
25   Itself for being there?

CAITHNESS
                              Well, march we on,
To give obedience where 'tis truly owed.
Meet we the medicine of the sickly weal,
And with him pour we in our country's purge
Each drop of us.

LENNOX
                              Or so much as it needs,
30   To dew the sovereign flower and drown the weeds.
Make we our march towards Birnam.

                              Exeunt, marching

MENTEITH

Who can blame him for acting crazy, when inside he condemns himself for everything he's done?

CAITHNESS

Well, let's keep marching and give our loyalty to someone who truly deserves it. We're going to meet Malcolm, the doctor who will cure our sick country. We'll pour out our own blood to help him.

LENNOX

However much blood we need to give to water the royal flower and drown the weeds—to make Malcolm king and get rid of Macbeth. Let's proceed on our march to Birnam.

They exit, marching.

ACT FIVE, Scene 3

Enter MACBETH, DOCTOR, *and attendants*

MACBETH
Bring me no more reports. Let them fly all.
Till Birnam Wood remove to Dunsinane
I cannot taint with fear. What's the boy Malcolm?
Was he not born of woman? The spirits that know
5   All mortal consequences have pronounced me thus:
"Fear not, Macbeth. No man that's born of woman
Shall e'er have power upon thee." Then fly, false thanes,
And mingle with the English epicures.
The mind I sway by and the heart I bear
10   Shall never sag with doubt nor shake with fear.

Enter a SERVANT

The devil damn thee black, thou cream-faced loon!
Where got'st thou that goose look?

SERVANT
There is ten thousand—

MACBETH
Geese, villain?

SERVANT
15   Soldiers, sir.

MACBETH
Go, prick thy face and over-red thy fear,
Thou lily-livered boy. What soldiers, patch?
Death of thy soul! Those linen cheeks of thine
Are counselors to fear. What soldiers, whey-face?

SERVANT
20   The English force, so please you.

MACBETH
Take thy face hence.

Exit SERVANT

ACT FIVE, Scene 3

MACBETH, *a* DOCTOR, *and attendants enter.*

MACBETH

Don't bring me any more reports. I don't care if all the thanes desert me. Until Birnam Wood gets up and moves to Dunsinane, I won't be affected by fear. What's the boy Malcolm? Wasn't he born from a woman? The spirits that know the future have told me this: "Don't be afraid, Macbeth. No man born from a woman will ever defeat you." So get out of here, disloyal thanes, and join the weak and decadent English! My mind and courage will never falter with doubt or shake with fear.

A SERVANT *enters.*

May the devil turn you black, you white-faced fool! Why do you look like a frightened goose?

SERVANT

There are ten thousand—

MACBETH

Geese, you idiot?

SERVANT

Soldiers, sir.

MACBETH

Go pinch your cheeks and bring some color back into your face, you cowardly boy. What soldiers, fool? Curse you! That pale face of yours will frighten the others as well. What soldiers, milk-face?

SERVANT

The English army, sir.

MACBETH

Get out of my sight.

The SERVANT *exits.*

                       Seyton!—I am sick at heart,
When I behold—Seyton, I say!—This push
Will cheer me ever, or disseat me now.
I have lived long enough. My way of life

25   Is fall'n into the sere, the yellow leaf,
And that which should accompany old age,
As honor, love, obedience, troops of friends,
I must not look to have, but, in their stead,
Curses, not loud but deep, mouth-honor, breath

30   Which the poor heart would fain deny and dare not.
Seyton!

Enter SEYTON

SEYTON
             What's your gracious pleasure?

MACBETH
                        What news more?

SEYTON
All is confirmed, my lord, which was reported.

MACBETH
I'll fight till from my bones my flesh be hacked.
Give me my armor.

SEYTON
35   'Tis not needed yet.

MACBETH
I'll put it on.
Send out more horses. Skirr the country round.
Hang those that talk of fear. Give me mine armor.
How does your patient, doctor?

DOCTOR
                    Not so sick, my lord,
40   As she is troubled with thick-coming fancies
That keep her from her rest.

Seyton!—I'm sick at heart when I see—Seyton, come here!—This battle will either secure my reign forever or else topple me from the throne. I have lived long enough. The course of my life is beginning to wither and fall away, like a yellowing leaf in autumn. The things that should go along with old age, like honor, love, obedience, and loyal friends, I cannot hope to have. Instead, I have passionate but quietly whispered curses, people who honor me with their words but not in their hearts, and lingering life, which my heart would gladly end, though I can't bring myself to do it. Seyton!

SEYTON *enters.*

SEYTON
What do you want?

MACBETH
Is there more news?

SEYTON
All the rumors have been confirmed.

MACBETH
I'll fight until they hack the flesh off my bones. Give me my armor.

SEYTON
You don't need it yet.

MACBETH
I'll put it on anyway. Send out more cavalry. Scour the whole country and hang anyone spreading fear. Give me my armor. *(to the* DOCTOR*)* How is my wife, doctor?

DOCTOR
She is not sick, my lord, but she is troubled with endless visions that keep her from sleeping.

MACBETH
                              Cure her of that.
Canst thou not minister to a mind diseased,
Pluck from the memory a rooted sorrow,
Raze out the written troubles of the brain
45   And with some sweet oblivious antidote
Cleanse the stuffed bosom of that perilous stuff
Which weighs upon the heart?

DOCTOR
                              Therein the patient
Must minister to himself.

MACBETH
Throw physic to the dogs; I'll none of it.
50   Come, put mine armor on. Give me my staff.
Seyton, send out.—Doctor, the thanes fly from me.
Come, sir, dispatch.—If thou couldst, doctor, cast
The water of my land, find her disease,
And purge it to a sound and pristine health,
55   I would applaud thee to the very echo,
That should applaud again.—Pull 't off, I say.—
What rhubarb, senna, or what purgative drug,
Would scour these English hence? Hear'st thou of them?

DOCTOR
Ay, my good lord. Your royal preparation
60   Makes us hear something.

MACBETH
                              Bring it after me.
I will not be afraid of death and bane,
Till Birnam Forest come to Dunsinane.

DOCTOR
(aside) Were I from Dunsinane away and clear,
Profit again should hardly draw me here.
                                        Exeunt

MACBETH

Cure her of that. Can't you treat a diseased mind? Take away her memory of sorrow? Use some drug to erase the troubling thoughts from her brain and ease her heart?

DOCTOR

For that kind of relief, the patient must heal herself.

MACBETH

Medicine is for the dogs. I won't have anything to do with it. *(to* SEYTON*)* Come, put my armor on me. Give me my lance. Seyton, send out the soldiers. *(to the* DOC-TOR*)* Doctor, the thanes are running away from me. *(to* SEYTON*)* Come on, sir, hurry. *(to the* DOCTOR*)* Can you figure out what's wrong with my country? If you can diagnose its disease by examining its urine, and bring it back to health, I will praise you to the ends of the Earth, where the sound will echo back so you can hear the applause again.—*(to* SEYTON*)* Pull it off, I tell you. *(to the* DOCTOR*)* What drug would purge the English from this country? Have you heard of any?

DOCTOR

Yes, my good lord. Your preparation for war sounds like something.

MACBETH

(to SEYTON*)* Bring the armor and follow me. I will not be afraid of death and destruction until Birnam forest picks itself up and moves to Dunsinane.

DOCTOR

(to himself) I wish I were far away from Dunsinane. You couldn't pay me to come back here.

They exit.

ACT FIVE, Scene 4

Drum and colors. Enter MALCOLM, SIWARD, MACDUFF, *Siward's* SON, MENTEITH, CAITHNESS, ANGUS, LENNOX, ROSS, *and* SOLDIERS, *marching*

MALCOLM
Cousins, I hope the days are near at hand
That chambers will be safe.

MENTEITH
We doubt it nothing.

SIWARD
What wood is this before us?

MENTEITH
The wood of Birnam.

MALCOLM
Let every soldier hew him down a bough
5   And bear 't before him. Thereby shall we shadow
The numbers of our host and make discovery
Err in report of us.

SOLDIERS
It shall be done.

SIWARD
We learn no other but the confident tyrant
Keeps still in Dunsinane and will endure
10   Our setting down before 't.

MALCOLM
'Tis his main hope:
For, where there is advantage to be given,
Both more and less have given him the revolt,
And none serve with him but constrainèd things
Whose hearts are absent too.

MACDUFF
Let our just censures
15   Attend the true event, and put we on
Industrious soldiership.

ACT FIVE, Scene 4

MALCOLM, *old* SIWARD *and his* SON, MACDUFF,
MENTEITH, CAITHNESS, ANGUS, LENNOX, ROSS, *and*
SOLDIERS *enter marching, with a drummer and flag.*

MALCOLM

Kinsmen, I hope the time is coming when people will
be safe in their own bedrooms.

MENTEITH

We don't doubt it.

SIWARD

What's the name of this forest behind us?

MENTEITH

Birnam Wood.

MALCOLM

Tell every soldier to break off a branch and hold it in
front of him. That way we can conceal how many of us
there are, and Macbeth's spies will give him inaccu-
rate reports.

SOLDIERS

We'll do it.

SIWARD

We have no news except that the overconfident Macbeth is still in Dunsinane and will allow us to lay siege
to the castle.

MALCOLM

He wants us to lay siege. Wherever his soldiers have
an opportunity to leave him, they do, whatever rank
they are. No one fights with him except men who are
forced to, and their hearts aren't in it.

MACDUFF

We shouldn't make any judgments until we achieve
our goal. Let's go fight like hardworking soldiers.

SIWARD
                          The time approaches
That will with due decision make us know
What we shall say we have and what we owe.
Thoughts speculative their unsure hopes relate,
20   But certain issue strokes must arbitrate.
Towards which, advance the war.

                                    Exeunt, marching

SIWARD

Soon we'll find out what's really ours and what isn't. It's easy for us to get our hopes up just sitting around thinking about it, but the only way this is really going to be settled is by violence. So let's move our armies forward.

They exit, marching.

ACT FIVE, Scene 5

Enter MACBETH, SEYTON, *and* SOLDIERS, *with drum and colors*

MACBETH
Hang out our banners on the outward walls.
The cry is still "They come!" Our castle's strength
Will laugh a siege to scorn. Here let them lie
Till famine and the ague eat them up.
5   Were they not forced with those that should be ours,
We might have met them dareful, beard to beard,
And beat them backward home.

A cry within of women

What is that noise?

SEYTON
It is the cry of women, my good lord.

Exit

MACBETH
I have almost forgot the taste of fears.
10   The time has been my senses would have cooled
To hear a night-shriek, and my fell of hair
Would at a dismal treatise rouse and stir
As life were in 't. I have supped full with horrors.
Direness, familiar to my slaughterous thoughts
15   Cannot once start me.

Enter SEYTON

Wherefore was that cry?

SEYTON
The queen, my lord, is dead.

ACT FIVE, Scene 5

MACBETH, SEYTON, *and* SOLDIERS *enter with a drummer and flag.*

MACBETH

Hang our flags on the outer walls. Everyone keeps yelling, "Here they come!" Our castle is strong enough to laugh off their seige. They can sit out there until they die of hunger and disease. If it weren't for the fact that so many of our soldiers revolted and joined them, we could have met them out in front of the castle, man to man, and beaten them back to England.

A sound of women crying offstage.

What's that noise?

SEYTON

It's women crying, my good lord.

SEYTON *exits.*

MACBETH

I've almost forgotten what fear feels like. There was a time when I would have been terrified by a shriek in the night, and the hair on my skin would have stood up when I heard a ghost story. But now I've had my fill of real horrors. Horrible things are so familiar that they can't startle me.

SEYTON *comes back in.*

What was that cry for?

SEYTON

The queen, is dead my lord.

MACBETH
She should have died hereafter.
There would have been a time for such a word.
Tomorrow, and tomorrow, and tomorrow,
20   Creeps in this petty pace from day to day
To the last syllable of recorded time,
And all our yesterdays have lighted fools
The way to dusty death. Out, out, brief candle!
Life's but a walking shadow, a poor player
25   That struts and frets his hour upon the stage
And then is heard no more. It is a tale
Told by an idiot, full of sound and fury,
Signifying nothing.

Enter a MESSENGER

Thou comest to use
Thy tongue; thy story quickly.

MESSENGER
Gracious my lord,
30   I should report that which I say I saw,
But know not how to do 't.

MACBETH
Well, say, sir.

MESSENGER
As I did stand my watch upon the hill,
I looked toward Birnam, and anon methought
The wood began to move.

MACBETH
Liar and slave!

MESSENGER
35   Let me endure your wrath, if 't be not so.
Within this three mile may you see it coming;
I say, a moving grove.

MACBETH

She would have died later anyway. That news was bound to come someday. Tomorrow, and tomorrow, and tomorrow. The days creep slowly along until the end of time. And every day that's already happened has taken fools that much closer to their deaths. Out, out, brief candle. Life is nothing more than an illusion. It's like a poor actor who struts and worries for his hour on the stage and then is never heard from again. Life is a story told by an idiot, full of noise and emotional disturbance but devoid of meaning.

A MESSENGER *enters.*

You've come to tell me something. Tell me quickly.

MESSENGER

My gracious lord, I should tell you what I saw, but I don't know how to say it.

MACBETH

Just say it.

MESSENGER

As I was standing watch on the hill, I looked toward Birnam, and I thought I saw the forest begin to move.

MACBETH

Liar and slave!

MESSENGER

Punish me if it's not true. Three miles from here you can see it coming, a moving forest.

ACT FIVE

MACBETH
       If thou speak'st false,
Upon the next tree shall thou hang alive
Till famine cling thee. If thy speech be sooth,
40 I care not if thou dost for me as much.
I pull in resolution and begin
To doubt th' equivocation of the fiend
That lies like truth. "Fear not, till Birnam wood
Do come to Dunsinane"; and now a wood
45 Comes toward Dunsinane.—Arm, arm, and out!—
If this which he avouches does appear,
There is nor flying hence nor tarrying here.
I 'gin to be aweary of the sun,
And wish th' estate o' th' world were now undone.—
50 Ring the alarum-bell!—Blow, wind! Come, wrack!
At least we'll die with harness on our back.
             Exeunt

MACBETH

If you're lying, I'll hang you alive from the nearest tree until you die of hunger. If what you say is true, you can do the same to me. *(to himself)* My confidence is failing. I'm starting to doubt the lies the devil told me, which sounded like truth. "Don't worry until Birnam Wood comes to Dunsinane." And now a wood is coming to Dunsinane. Prepare for battle, and go! If what this messenger says is true, it's no use running away or staying here. I'm starting to grow tired of living, and I'd like to see the world plunged into chaos. Ring the alarms! Blow, wind! Come, ruin! At least we'll die with our armor on.

They exit.

ACT FIVE, Scene 6

Drum and colors. Enter MALCOLM, SIWARD, MACDUFF, *and their army, with boughs*

MALCOLM
　Now near enough. Your leafy screens throw down,
　And show like those you are.—You, worthy uncle,
　Shall, with my cousin, your right-noble son,
　Lead our first battle. Worthy Macduff and we
5　Shall take upon 's what else remains to do,
　According to our order.

SIWARD
　　　　　　　　　Fare you well.
　Do we but find the tyrant's power tonight,
　Let us be beaten if we cannot fight.

MACDUFF
10　Make all our trumpets speak; give them all breath,
　Those clamorous harbingers of blood and death.

　　　　　　　　　　　　　　　　　Exeunt

ACT FIVE, Scene 6

MALCOLM, *old* SIWARD, MACDUFF, *and their army enter carrying branches, with a drummer and flag.*

MALCOLM

We're close enough now. Throw down these branches and show them who you really are. Uncle Siward, you and your son will lead the first battle. Brave Macduff and I will do the rest, according to our battle plan.

SIWARD

Good luck. If we meet Macbeth's army tonight, let us be beaten if we cannot fight.

MACDUFF

Blow all the trumpets. They loudly announce the news of blood and death.

They exit.

ACT FIVE, Scene 7

Alarums. Enter MACBETH

MACBETH
They have tied me to a stake. I cannot fly,
But, bearlike, I must fight the course. What's he
That was not born of woman? Such a one
Am I to fear, or none.

Enter YOUNG SIWARD

YOUNG SIWARD
5   What is thy name?
MACBETH
Thou 'lt be afraid to hear it.
YOUNG SIWARD
No, though thou call'st thyself a hotter name
Than any is in hell.
MACBETH
My name's Macbeth.
YOUNG SIWARD
The devil himself could not pronounce a title
10   More hateful to mine ear.
MACBETH
No, nor more fearful.
YOUNG SIWARD
Thou liest, abhorrèd tyrant. With my sword
I'll prove the lie thou speak'st.

They fight and YOUNG SIWARD *is slain*

MACBETH
Thou wast born of woman. But swords I smile at,
weapons laugh to scorn, Brandished by man that's
of a woman born.

ACT FIVE, Scene 7

Trumpets and the noise of battle. MACBETH *enters.*

MACBETH

In Shakespeare's time, bears were tied to stakes and attacked by dogs for the amusement of audiences.

They have me tied to a stake. I can't run away. I have to stand and fight, like a bear. Where's the man who wasn't born from a woman? He's the only one I'm afraid of, nobody else.

YOUNG SIWARD *enters.*

YOUNG SIWARD
What's your name?

MACBETH
You'll be afraid to hear it.

YOUNG SIWARD
No I won't, even if you were one of the worst demons in hell.

MACBETH
My name's Macbeth.

YOUNG SIWARD
The devil himself couldn't say a name I hate more.

MACBETH
No, nor could the devil's name be more frightening.

YOUNG SIWARD
You lie, you disgusting tyrant. I'll prove with my sword that I'm not scared of you.

They fight and YOUNG SIWARD *is killed.*

MACBETH
You were born from a woman. Swords don't frighten me. I laugh at any weapon used by a man who was born from a woman.

Exit

Alarums. Enter MACDUFF

MACDUFF
15   That way the noise is. Tyrant, show thy face!
        If thou beest slain, and with no stroke of mine,
        My wife and children's ghosts will haunt me still.
        I cannot strike at wretched kerns, whose arms
        Are hired to bear their staves. Either thou, Macbeth,
20   Or else my sword with an unbattered edge
        I sheathe again undeeded. There thou shouldst be;
        By this great clatter, one of the greatest note
        Seems bruited. Let me find him, Fortune,
        And more I beg not.
                                    Exit. Alarums
        Enter MALCOLM *and* SIWARD

SIWARD
25   This way, my lord. The castle's gently rendered.
        The tyrant's people on both sides do fight,
        The noble thanes do bravely in the war,
        The day almost itself professes yours,
        And little is to do.
MALCOLM
                        We have met with foes
30   That strike beside us.
SIWARD
        Enter, sir, the castle.
                                    Exeunt. Alarums

MACBETH *exits.*

Trumpets and battle sounds. MACDUFF *enters.*

MACDUFF

The noise is coming from over there. Tyrant, show your face! If someone other than me kills you, the ghosts of my wife and children will haunt me forever. I can't be bothered to fight these lame soldiers who only fight for money. I'll either fight you, Macbeth, or else I'll put down my sword unused. You must be over there. By the great noise, it sounds like one of the highest-ranking men is being announced. I hope I find him! I ask for nothing more than that.

MACDUFF *exits. More battle noises.*

MALCOLM *and old* SIWARD *enter.*

SIWARD

Come this way, my lord. The castle has been surrendered without a fight. Macbeth's soldiers are fighting on both sides. Our noblemen are battling bravely. The victory is almost yours, and it seems like there's not much left to do.

MALCOLM

Our enemies fight as if they're trying not to hurt us.

SIWARD

Sir, enter the castle.

They exit. Battle noises continue.

ACT FIVE, Scene 8

Enter MACBETH

MACBETH

Why should I play the Roman fool and die
On mine own sword? Whiles I see lives, the gashes
Do better upon them.

Enter MACDUFF

MACDUFF

Turn, hellhound, turn!

MACBETH

Of all men else I have avoided thee.
5   But get thee back. My soul is too much charged
With blood of thine already.

MACDUFF

I have no words. My voice is in my sword.
Thou bloodier villain Than terms can give
thee out!

They fight

MACBETH

Thou losest labor. As easy mayst thou the
intrenchant air. With thy keen sword impress as
10   make me bleed. Let fall thy blade on vulnerable
crests; I bear a charmèd life, which must not
yield to one of woman born.

MACDUFF

Despair thy charm, And let the angel whom
thou still hast served Tell thee, Macduff was
15   from his mother's womb Untimely ripped.

ACT FIVE, Scene 8

MACBETH *enters.*

MACBETH

Why should I commit suicide like one of the ancient Romans? As long as I see enemies of mine alive, I would rather see my sword wound them than me.

MACDUFF *enters.*

MACDUFF

Turn around, you dog from hell, turn around!

MACBETH

You are the only man I have avoided. But go away now. I'm already guilty of killing your whole family.

MACDUFF

I have nothing to say to you. My sword will talk for me. You are too evil for words!

They fight.

MACBETH

You're wasting your time trying to wound me. You might as well try to stab the air with your sword. Go fight someone who can be harmed. I lead a charmed life, which can't be ended by anyone born from a woman.

MACDUFF

You can forget about your charm. The evil spirit you serve can tell you that I was not born. They cut me out of my mother's womb before she could bear me naturally.

MACBETH
Accursèd be that tongue that tells me so,
For it hath cowed my better part of man!
And be these juggling fiends no more believed,
20   That palter with us in a double sense,
That keep the word of promise to our ear,
And break it to our hope. I'll not fight with thee.

MACDUFF
Then yield thee, coward,
And live to be the show and gaze o' th' time.
25   We'll have thee, as our rarer monsters are,
Painted on a pole, and underwrit,
"Here may you see the tyrant."

MACBETH
I will not yield,
To kiss the ground before young Malcolm's feet,
And to be baited with the rabble's curse.
30   Though Birnam Wood be come to Dunsinane,
And thou opposed, being of no woman born,
Yet I will try the last. Before my body
I throw my warlike shield. Lay on, Macduff,
And damned be him that first cries, "Hold, enough!"

Exeunt, fighting. Alarums. They enter fighting, and
MACBETH *slain. Retreat. Flourish. Enter, with drum and*
colors MALCOLM, SIWARD, ROSS, THANES, *and* SOLDIERS

MALCOLM
35   I would the friends we miss were safe arrived.

SIWARD
Some must go off. And yet, by these I see,
So great a day as this is cheaply bought.

MALCOLM
Macduff is missing, and your noble son.

MACBETH

Curse you for telling me this. You've fightened away my courage. I don't believe those evil creatures anymore. They tricked me with their wordgames, raising my hopes and then destroying them. I won't fight you.

MACDUFF

Then surrender, coward, and we'll put you in a freakshow, just like they do with deformed animals. We'll put a picture of you on a sign, right above the words "Come see the tyrant!"

MACBETH

I'm not going to surrender and have to kiss the ground in front of Malcolm, or be taunted by the common people. Even though Birnam Wood really did come to Dunsinane, and I'm fighting a man not of woman born, I'll fight to the end. I'll put up my shield and battle you. Come on, let's go at it, Macduff, and damn the first man who cries, 'Stop! Enough!'

They exit fighting. Trumpets and battle noises. The trumpet of one army sounds a call to retreat. Macbeth is killed. The other army's trumpet sounds a call of victory. The victorious army enters, led by MALCOLM, *old* SIWARD, ROSS, *the other* THANES, *and soldiers, with a drummer and flag.*

MALCOLM

I wish all of our friends could have survived this battle.

SIWARD

In every battle, some people will always be killed, but judging from the men I see around us, our great victory didn't cost us very much.

MALCOLM

Macduff is missing, and so is your noble son.

ACT FIVE

ROSS
   Your son, my lord, has paid a soldier's debt.
40 He only lived but till he was a man,
   The which no sooner had his prowess confirmed
   In the unshrinking station where he fought,
   But like a man he died.

SIWARD
                              Then he is dead?

ROSS
   Ay, and brought off the field. Your cause of sorrow
45 Must not be measured by his worth, for then
   It hath no end.

SIWARD
                        Had he his hurts before?

ROSS
   Ay, on the front.

SIWARD
                              Why then, God's soldier be he!
   Had I as many sons as I have hairs,
   I would not wish them to a fairer death.
50 And so, his knell is knolled.

MALCOLM
                                       He's worth more sorrow,
   And that I'll spend for him.

SIWARD
                                       He's worth no more.
   They say he parted well and paid his score.
   And so, God be with him! Here comes newer comfort.

   Enter MACDUFF *with* MACBETH'S *head*

MACDUFF
   Hail, king! For so thou art. Behold where stands
55 The usurper's cursèd head. The time is free.
   I see thee compassed with thy kingdom's pearl,
   That speak my salutation in their minds,

ROSS

My lord, your son has paid the soldier's price: death. He only lived long enough to become a man, and as soon as he proved that he was a man by fighting like one, he died.

SIWARD

So he's dead?

ROSS

Yes, and he's been carried off the field. Your grief should not be equal to his worth, because then your sorrow would never end.

SIWARD

Were his wounds on his front side?

ROSS

Yes, on his front.

SIWARD

Well then, he's God's soldier now! If I had as many sons as I have hairs on my head, I couldn't hope that any of them would die more honorably than he did. And that's all there is to it.

MALCOLM

He is worth more mourning than that, and I will mourn for him.

SIWARD

He is worth no more than that. They tell me he died well, and settled his scores. With that, I hope God is with him! Here comes better news.

MACDUFF *enters, carrying* MACBETH'S *head.*

MACDUFF

Hail, king! Because that's what you are now. Look, here I have Macbeth's cursed head. We are free from his tyranny. I see that you have the kingdom's noblemen around you, and they're thinking the same thing

Whose voices I desire aloud with mine.
Hail, King of Scotland!

ALL
                        Hail, King of Scotland!

Flourish

MALCOLM
60   We shall not spend a large expense of time
        Before we reckon with your several loves
        And make us even with you. My thanes and kinsmen,
        Henceforth be earls, the first that ever Scotland
        In such an honor named. What's more to do,
65   Which would be planted newly with the time,
        As calling home our exiled friends abroad
        That fled the snares of watchful tyranny,
        Producing forth the cruel ministers
        Of this dead butcher and his fiendlike queen,
70   Who, as 'tis thought, by self and violent hands
        Took off her life; this, and what needful else
        That calls upon us, by the grace of Grace,
        We will perform in measure, time, and place.
        So, thanks to all at once and to each one,
75   Whom we invite to see us crowned at Scone.
                                    Flourish. Exeunt

as me. I want them to join me in this loud cheer, Hail, King of Scotland!

ALL

Hail, King of Scotland!

Trumpets play.

MALCOLM

It won't be long before I reward each of you as he deserves. My thanes and kinsmen, I name you all earls, the first earls that Scotland has ever had. We have a lot to do at the dawn of this new era. We must call home all of our exiled friends who fled from the grip of Macbeth's tyranny, and we must bring to justice all the evil ministers of this dead butcher and his demon-like queen, who, rumor has it, committed suicide. This, and whatever else we are called to do by God, we will do at the right time and in the right place. So I thank you all, and I invite each and every one of you to come watch me be crowned king of Scotland at Scone.

Trumpets play. They all exit.

PART III

STUDY
GUIDE

6

THEMATIC QUESTIONS

1) Characterize the relationship between Macbeth and Lady Macbeth. If the main theme of *Macbeth* is ambition, whose ambition is the driving force of the play—Macbeth's, Lady Macbeth's, or both?

The Macbeths' marriage, like the couple themselves, is atypical, particularly by the standards of its time. Yet despite their odd power dynamic, the two of them seem surprisingly attached to one another, particularly compared to other married couples in Shakespeare's plays, in which romantic felicity appears primarily during courtship and marriages tend to be troubled. Macbeth offers an exception to this rule, as Macbeth and his wife are partners in the truest sense of the word. Of course, the irony of their "happy" marriage is clear—they are united by their crimes, their mutual madness, and their mounting alienation from the rest of humanity.

Though Macbeth is a brave general and a powerful lord, his wife is far from subordinate to his will. Indeed, she often seems to control him, either by crafty manipulation or by direct order. And it is Lady Macbeth's deep-seated ambition, rather than her husband's, that ultimately propels the plot of the play by goading Macbeth to murder Duncan. Macbeth does not need any help coming up with the idea of murdering Duncan, but it seems unlikely that he would have committed the murder without his wife's powerful taunts and persuasions.

2) One of the important themes in *Macbeth* is the idea of political legitimacy, of the moral authority that some kings possess and others lack. With particular attention to Malcolm's questioning of Macduff in Act IV, Scene 3, try to define some of the characteristics that grant or invalidate the moral legitimacy of absolute power. What makes Duncan a good king? What makes Macbeth a tyrant?

After Duncan's death, the nobles of Scotland begin to grumble among themselves about what they perceive as Macbeth's tyrannical behavior. When Macduff meets Malcolm in England, Malcolm pretends that he would make an even worse king than Macbeth in order to test Macduff's loyalty to Scotland. The bad qualities he claims to possess include lust, greed, and a chaotic and violent temperament. These qualities all seem characteristic of Macbeth, whereas Duncan's universally lauded reign was marked by the king's kindness, generosity, and stabilizing presence. The king must be able to keep order and should reward his subjects according to their merits. For example, Duncan makes Macbeth thane of Cawdor after Macbeth's victory over the invaders. Perhaps the most important quality of a true king to emerge in Malcolm's conversation with Macduff is loyalty to Scotland and its people above oneself. Macbeth wishes to be king to gratify his own desires, while Duncan and Malcolm wear the crown out of love for their nation.

3) An important theme in *Macbeth* is the relationship between gender and power, particularly Shakespeare's exploration of the values that make up the idea of masculinity. What are these values, and how do various characters embody them? How does Shakespeare subvert his characters' perception of gender roles?

Manhood, for most of the characters in *Macbeth*, is tied to ideals of strength, power, physical courage, and force of will; it is rarely tied to ideals of intelligence or moral fortitude. At several points in the play, the characters goad one another into action by questioning each other's manhood. Most significantly, Lady Macbeth emasculates her husband repeatedly, knowing that in his desperation to prove his manhood he will perform the acts she wishes him to perform. Macbeth echoes Lady Macbeth's words when he questions the manhood of the murderers he has hired to kill Banquo, and after Macduff's wife and children are killed, Malcolm urges Macduff to take the news with manly reserve and to devote himself to the destruction of Macbeth, his family's murderer. Ultimately, there is a strong suggestion that manhood is tied to cruelty and violence: note Lady Macbeth's speech in Act I, Scene 5, when she asks to be "unsexed" so that she can help her husband commit murder. Yet, at the same time, the audience is clearly meant to realize that women provide the push that sets the bloody action of the play in motion. Macduff, too, suggests that the equation of masculinity with cruelty is not quite correct. His comments show that he believes emotion and reflection are also important attributes of the true man.

7

KEY QUESTIONS
AND ANSWERS

1. Are the witches in *Macbeth* real?

Yes. Macbeth really does see the three witches in the play. Banquo also sees them and speaks with them. Initially, Banquo questions the witches about whether they are real or possibly a hallucination he and Macbeth both share, but throughout the rest of the play both men seem to accept the witches as physical beings. Later in the play, the witches appear with their queen, Hecate, in a scene without any human characters. If Macbeth had been hallucinating the witches, he would need to be onstage for them to be seen. He is not, which is more proof that in the world of this play, they are real. We can also contrast the treatment of the witches to Banquo's ghost. When Macbeth claims he sees the ghost, Lady Macbeth insists she doesn't see anything, telling Macbeth "When all's done/ You look but on a stool." (III.vi.) In the play, both Macbeth and his wife have hallucinations that they alone see, but the witches are clearly visible to more than just Macbeth.

2. Did Macbeth always want to be king?

The audience sees Macbeth for the first time just moments before he and Banquo encounter the witches. Thus, there's not much time for the audience to learn anything about Macbeth before the witches' prophesy. However, immediately upon hearing that he will be king, Macbeth seems to have a strong reaction, causing Banquo to say "Good sir, why do you start and seem to fear/ Things that do sound so fair?" (I.iii.) Macbeth's reaction suggests he has powerful feelings about the prospect of being king. Similarly, when Lady Macbeth reads a letter from Macbeth telling of the prophecies for his future, she immediately begins to plot to kill Duncan and take the throne, suggesting that Lady Macbeth has also always dreamed of being queen.

3. **Why does Macbeth think the witches want to help him?**

When Malcom reveals that he was taken from his mother's womb—or, in other words, delivered via Cesarean section—Macbeth finally understands that the witches' prophecies meant his downfall, not his elevation. Up to the end of the play, Macbeth has confused the fact that the witches' predictions always came true with the idea that their predictions were helpful to him. Everything the witches predict does come true, but everything that happens ends up hurting Macbeth as well. He does become thane of Cawdor, but that feeds his ambition so he kills Duncan. He becomes the king, but as a result kills many people, including his best friend. When Macbeth hears the witches' final prediction, he is tormented by the vision of Banquo's children ruling instead of him, but he still doesn't understand that the witches are not on his side. He sees their predictions that he can't be defeated until Birnam Wood moves and that he can't be killed except by a man not born of a woman as proof that he is protected. He is very wrong.

4. Does Lady Macbeth commit suicide?

Shakespeare leaves the exact nature of Lady Macbeth's death ambiguous. When Macbeth is told that his wife has died, no details are given and he does not ask for them. Instead, he talks about how futile and pointless life is. At the end of the play, Malcolm tells the noblemen that "'tis thought, by self and violent hands" the queen killed herself, but the inclusion of the word "thought" implies her suicide is a rumor. Suicide is considered a mortal sin by the Roman Catholic Church and thus frowned upon throughout England. According to church law, if Lady Macbeth killed herself, she would be eternally damned. Yet the question is never fully answered.

5. How did Birnam Wood move and why was Macduff able to kill Macbeth?

When Malcolm, Macduff, Siward, and the other nobles are planning to attack Macbeth's castle and overthrow him, in Act V, Scene 4, they are in Birnam Wood, across the fields. Malcolm orders the soldiers to break off boughs from the trees in the wood, and hold the boughs in front of them as they march toward Macbeth. He says that doing so will conceal their true numbers from those watching for Macbeth, who will not be able to report an accurate count to the king. From Macbeth's perspective, many yards away, it does look like the Birnam Wood itself is moving when the men do this. Although the witches tell Macbeth he cannot be killed by a man "of woman born," Macduff reveals to Macbeth that he was delivered by what we call a Cesarean section, cut out of his mother's body instead of being born in the more usual manner. Thus, Macduff fulfills the witches' prediction that a man not born of a woman is the only person who can kill Macbeth.

NOTES

NOTES

THEMES, MOTIFS, AND SYMBOLS

Themes

Themes are the fundamental and often universal ideas explored in a literary work.

THE CORRUPTING POWER OF UNCHECKED AMBITION

The main theme of *Macbeth*—the destruction wrought when ambition goes unchecked by moral constraints—finds its most powerful expression in the play's two main characters. Macbeth is a courageous Scottish general who is not naturally inclined to commit evil deeds, yet he deeply desires power and advancement. He kills Duncan against his better judgment and afterward stews in guilt and paranoia. Toward the end of the play he descends into a kind of frantic, boastful madness. Lady Macbeth, on the other hand, pursues her goals with greater determination, yet she is less capable of withstanding the repercussions of her immoral acts. One of Shakespeare's most forcefully drawn female characters, she spurs her husband mercilessly to kill Duncan and urges him to be strong in the murder's aftermath, but she is eventually driven to distraction by the effect of Macbeth's repeated bloodshed on her conscience. In each case, ambition—helped, of course, by the malign prophecies of the witches—is what drives the couple to ever more terrible atrocities. The problem, the play suggests, is that once one decides to use violence to further one's quest for power, it is difficult to stop. There are always potential threats to the throne—Banquo, Fleance, Macduff—and it is always tempting to use violent means to dispose of them.

THE RELATIONSHIP BETWEEN CRUELTY
AND MASCULINITY

Characters in *Macbeth* frequently dwell on issues of gender. Lady Macbeth manipulates her husband by questioning his manhood, wishes that she herself could be "unsexed," and does not contradict Macbeth when he says that a woman like her should give birth only to boys. In the same manner that Lady Macbeth goads her husband on to murder, Macbeth provokes the murderers he hires to kill Banquo by questioning their manhood. Such acts show that both Macbeth and Lady Macbeth equate masculinity with naked aggression, and whenever they converse about manhood, violence soon follows. Their understanding of manhood allows the political order depicted in the play to descend into chaos.

At the same time, however, the audience cannot help noticing that women are also sources of violence and evil. The witches' prophecies spark Macbeth's ambitions and then encourage his violent behavior; Lady Macbeth provides the brains and the will behind her husband's plotting; and the only divine being to appear is Hecate, the goddess of witchcraft. Arguably, *Macbeth* traces the root of chaos and evil to women, which has led some critics to argue that this is Shakespeare's most misogynistic play. While the male characters are just as violent and prone to evil as the women, the aggression of the female characters is more striking because it goes against prevailing expectations of how women ought to behave. Lady Macbeth's behavior certainly shows that women can be as ambitious and cruel as men. Whether because of the constraints of her society or because she is not fearless enough to kill, Lady Macbeth relies on deception and manipulation rather than violence to achieve her ends.

Ultimately, the play does put forth a revised and less destructive definition of manhood. In the scene where Macduff learns of the murders of his wife and children, Malcolm consoles him by encouraging him to take the news in "manly" fashion, by seeking revenge upon Macbeth. Macduff shows the young heir apparent that he has a mistaken understanding of masculinity. To Malcolm's suggestion, "Dispute it like a man," Macduff replies, "I shall do so.

But I must also feel it as a man" (IV.iii.). At the end of the play, Siward receives news of his son's death rather complacently. Malcolm responds: "He's worth more sorrow [than you have expressed] / And that I'll spend for him" (V.xi.). Malcolm's comment shows that he has learned the lesson Macduff gave him on the sentient nature of true masculinity. It also suggests that, with Malcolm's coronation, order will be restored to the kingdom of Scotland.

THE DIFFERENCE BETWEEN KINGSHIP AND TYRANNY

In the play, Duncan is always referred to as a "king," while Macbeth soon becomes known as the "tyrant." The difference between the two types of rulers seems to be expressed in a conversation that occurs in Act IV, Scene 3, when Macduff meets Malcolm in England. In order to test Macduff's loyalty to Scotland, Malcolm pretends that he would make an even worse king than Macbeth. He tells Macduff of his reproachable qualities—among them a thirst for personal power and a violent temperament, both of which seem to characterize Macbeth perfectly. On the other hand, Malcolm says, "The king-becoming graces / [are] justice, verity, temp'rance, stableness, / Bounty, perseverance, mercy, [and] lowliness" (IV.iii.). The model king, then, offers the kingdom an embodiment of order and justice, but also comfort and affection. Under him, subjects are rewarded according to their merits, as when Duncan makes Macbeth thane of Cawdor after Macbeth's victory over the invaders. Most important, the king must be loyal to Scotland above his own interests. Macbeth, by contrast, brings only chaos to Scotland—symbolized in the bad weather and bizarre supernatural events—and offers no real justice, only a habit of capriciously murdering those he sees as a threat. As the embodiment of tyranny, he must be overcome by Malcolm so that Scotland can have a true king once more.

Motifs

Motifs are recurring structures, contrasts, and literary devices that can help to develop and inform the text's major themes.

HALLUCINATIONS

Visions and hallucinations recur throughout the play and serve as reminders of Macbeth and Lady Macbeth's joint culpability for the growing body count. When he is about to kill Duncan, Macbeth sees a dagger floating in the air. Covered with blood and pointed toward the king's chamber, the dagger represents the bloody course on which Macbeth is about to embark. Later, he sees Banquo's ghost sitting in a chair at a feast, pricking his conscience by mutely reminding him that he murdered his former friend. The seemingly hardheaded Lady Macbeth also eventually gives way to visions, as she sleepwalks and believes that her hands are stained with blood that cannot be washed away by any amount of water. In each case, it is ambiguous whether the vision is real or purely hallucinatory; but, in both cases, the Macbeths read them uniformly as supernatural signs of their guilt.

VIOLENCE

Macbeth is a famously violent play. Interestingly, most of the killings take place offstage, but throughout the play the characters provide the audience with gory descriptions of the carnage, from the opening scene where the captain describes Macbeth and Banquo wading in blood on the battlefield, to the endless references to the bloodstained hands of Macbeth and his wife. The action is bookended by a pair of bloody battles: in the first, Macbeth defeats the invaders; in the second, he is slain and beheaded by Macduff. In between is a series of murders: Duncan, Duncan's chamberlains, Banquo, Lady Macduff, and Macduff's son all come to bloody ends. By the end of the action, blood seems to be everywhere.

PROPHECY

Prophecy sets *Macbeth*'s plot in motion—namely, the witches' prophecy that Macbeth will become first thane of Cawdor and then king. The weird sisters make a number of other prophecies: They tell us that Banquo's heirs will be kings, that Macbeth should beware Macduff, that Macbeth is safe until Birnam Wood comes to Dunsinane, and that no man born of woman can harm Macbeth. Save for the prophecy about Banquo's heirs, all of these predictions are fulfilled within the course of the play. Still, it is left deliberately ambiguous whether some of them are self-fulfilling—for example, whether Macbeth wills himself to be king or is fated to be king. Additionally, as the Birnam Wood and "born of woman" prophecies make clear, the prophecies must be interpreted as riddles, since they do not always mean what they seem to mean.

Symbols

Symbols are objects, characters, figures, and colors used to represent abstract ideas or concepts.

BLOOD

Blood is everywhere in *Macbeth*, beginning with the opening battle between the Scots and the Norwegian invaders, which is described in harrowing terms by the wounded captain in Act I, Scene 2. Once Macbeth and Lady Macbeth embark upon their murderous journey, blood comes to symbolize their guilt, and they begin to feel that their crimes have stained them in a way that cannot be washed clean. "Will all great Neptune's ocean wash this blood / Clean from my hand?" Macbeth cries after he has killed Duncan, even as his wife scolds him and says that a little water will do the job (II.ii.). Later, though, she comes to share his horrified sense of being stained: "Out, damned spot; out, I say . . . who would have thought the old man to have had so much blood in him?" she asks as she wanders through the halls of their castle near the close of the play (V.i.). Blood symbolizes the guilt that sits like a permanent stain on the consciences of both Macbeth and Lady Macbeth, one that hounds them to their graves.

THE WEATHER

As in other Shakespearean tragedies, *Macbeth*'s grotesque murder spree is accompanied by a number of unnatural occurrences in the natural realm. From the thunder and lightning that accompany the witches' appearances to the terrible storms that rage on the night of Duncan's murder, these violations of the natural order reflect corruption in the moral and political orders.

9

QUOTES AND ANALYSIS
BY THEME

AMBITION

Two truths are told

As happy prologues to the swelling act

Of th'imperial theme

(I.iii.)

Macbeth speaks these lines as he realizes that the witches' prophecy (that he will be thane of Cawdor) has come true. He immediately starts to wonder whether this means that their third prophecy
(that he will become king) will also be true. The eagerness with
which he turns to this idea suggests that he finds the possibility
appealing, even though he also realizes he would have to commit
a terrible and violent act in order to achieve the position. These
lines hint at Macbeth's ambition and foreshadow his later actions
even though, at this point in the play, he seems to refuse to consider
acting upon it.

Thou wouldst be great

Art not without ambition, but without

The illness should attend it

(I.v.)

Lady Macbeth speaks these lines as she reflects on her
husband's character. She knows that Macbeth is capable of
ambitious dreams, but she thinks that he is unwilling to display the
ruthless behavior necessary to achieve those dreams. These lines
reflect Lady Macbeth's own philosophy of power, in which only
individuals who are willing to set their morality aside will rise to

greatness. They also show that she is a sound judge of character and understands her husband very well.

> *I have no spur*
>
> *To prick the sides of my intent, but only*
>
> *Vaulting ambition, which o'erleaps itself*
>
> *And falls on th'other*
>
> *(I.vii.)*

Macbeth speaks these lines as he starts to doubt his plan to murder Duncan. He uses a complicated metaphor that compares his experience to horse-riding. He describes being unable to motivate himself to take action by likening himself to a rider who cannot use his spurs to motivate his horse to go faster. The one thing he does have is ambition, which he compares to a horse and rider who overestimate their ability to leap over an obstacle and end up falling down. The passage describes the tension between Macbeth's unwillingness to move ahead with his plan and his acknowledgement that his ambition is leading him down a dangerous path.

GUILT

> *Will all great Neptune's ocean wash this blood*
>
> *Clean from my hand? No, this my hand will rather*
>
> *The multitudinous seas incarnadine*
>
> *(II.ii.)*

Macbeth speaks this line when he encounters his wife right after murdering Duncan. He refers to both the literal blood on his hand but also to his sense of guilt. He uses grand and dramatic language to imply that the blood could stain all the world's oceans red. His language implies that the consequences of his action will not be easily hidden, even though his wife implies that blood can be simply washed away. He will forever be a changed man as a result of what he has done. Interestingly, later in the play, Lady Macbeth will also hallucinate that she has blood on her hands and is unable to get them clean, symbolizing her sense of guilt.

Thy bones are marrowless, thy blood is cold

Thou hast no speculation in those eyes

(III.iv.)

Macbeth speaks this line when Banquo's ghost appears to him at the banquet. Macbeth's vision of the ghost reveals his guilt over ordering the murder of Banquo and his young son. His sense of guilt is so powerful that he loses his sense of reality and cannot be sure whether he is having a vision or not. He speaks these lines in order to try and reassure himself that Banquo is truly dead. In doing so, Macbeth reveals that his tormented consciousness is leading him to start losing his grip on sanity.

To bed, to bed. There's knocking at the gate.

Come, come, come, come, give me your hand.

What's done cannot be undone. To bed, to bed, to bed.

(V.i.)

Lady Macbeth speaks these lines after she has gone mad. They are the final words she utters in the play, and they reveal how guilt has crushed her strong and assertive personality. She now has to be cared for like a child and has no plans for the future. Her acknowledgement that the past cannot be changed reveals that there is no cure for guilt and regret. No matter how much she repents, the violence and death cannot be undone.

CHILDREN

I have given suck, and know

How tender 'tis to love the babe that milks me

I would, while it was smiling in my face

Have plucked my nipple from his boneless gums

And dashed the brains out

(I.vii.)

Lady Macbeth speaks these lines when she is trying to shame Macbeth for questioning their plan. She uses the image of a child to make a graphic statement about her own ambition and capacity for violence. By describing herself as a tender and loving mother who nonetheless would have killed her own child before she would abort a plan to seize power, Lady Macbeth disrupts the typical idea of what women and mothers are like. She uses this image to tell her husband that he is being unmanly by doubting their scheme.

> *For Banquo's issue have I filed my mind*
> *For them the gracious Duncan have I murdered*
> *(III.i.)*

Macbeth speaks these lines when he is brooding about his worries that, as the witches have prophesied, Banquo's heirs will someday gain control of the Scottish crown. Macbeth reveals that he feels guilty about the terrible things he has done and that he is wondering if these acts were worthwhile. Even though he currently holds power, Macbeth lacks children who will hold power after him and this makes him fear that he has committed terrible deeds for no reason. These lines speak to a strong interest in stable succession, which was a key political issue in Shakespeare's time.

> *What, all my pretty chickens and their dam*
> *At one fell swoop*
> *(IV.iii.)*

Macduff speaks these tragic lines upon learning that his wife and children have been murdered. The affectionate imagery he uses to describe them shows how even though he is a strong and powerful warrior, he is also a loving husband and father. The line conveys the sense of overwhelming loss he feels when he hears that he has lost his entire family at the same time. The sense of immense grief sets the stage for his desire to avenge them by eventually killing Macbeth.

PATRIOTISM

Every one did bear
Thy praises in his kingdom's great defense
(I.iii.)

This line is spoken by Ross to Macbeth, explaining how pleased Duncan was with the bravery Macbeth showed during the rebellion. Ross highlights that Macbeth showed solidarity and patriotism for defending Scotland against a usurper and indicates that these qualities make Macbeth worthy of praise and honor. The line, however, will later turn out to be ironic in that Macbeth will be revealed to be someone whom Scotland needs to be defended against.

Our duties are to your throne and state children
and servants
(I.v.)

Macbeth speaks this line to Duncan, expressing the high level of loyalty and devotion a good subject should feel toward his king. The line reveals how a king and the nation that king rules are intertwined, and how someone who is loyal to one should be loyal to the other. However, this line also reveals that patriotism and loyalty can be feigned, since Macbeth is planning to kill Duncan and usurp the throne even as he is seemingly showing how obedient he is.

Bleed, bleed, poor country!
(IV.iii.)

Macduff speaks this line when he thinks he will not be able to persuade Malcolm to fight against Macbeth and take back the throne. He is in despair, and his main concern is the suffering that Scotland and his people will experience while Macbeth remains on the throne. Macduff shows his patriotism and devotion to his country by lamenting the fate he is afraid it will be left to suffer.

10

QUOTES AND ANALYSIS BY CHARACTER

MACBETH

Is this a dagger which I see before me,
This handle toward my hand? Come, let me clutch thee.
I have thee not, and yet I see thee still.
Art thou not, fatal vision, sensible
To feeling as to sight? Or art thou but
A dagger of the mind, a false creation,
Proceeding from the heat-oppressèd brain?
(II.i.)

Macbeth's soliloquy is important as it marks the first time he hallucinates. We can assume the witches he saw earlier were real because Banquo saw them too. In these lines, however, Macbeth is aware that the floating knife he sees is not really there. The fact that he is troubled enough to hallucinate, yet still sane enough to understand that he is hallucinating, can be contrasted with his later mental state, when he fully believes he sees Banquo's ghost, even though Lady Macbeth tells him no one is there.

Whence is that knocking? –
How is't with me, when every noise appalls me?
What hands are here! Ha, they pluck out mine eyes.
Will all great Neptune's ocean wash this blood
Clean from my hand? No, this my hand will rather

The multitudinous seas incarnadine,

Making the green one red.

(II.ii.)

Macbeth says these lines immediately after murdering Duncan. He hears a knocking at the gate to the castle and thinks it must be his doom coming to claim him. This moment, now that the dreadful deed is done, shows Macbeth what the rest of his life will be like: He will become king, but he also will be wracked with guilt and sure that supernatural elements are warning him of his imminent death.

It will have blood, they say. Blood will have blood.

Stones have been known to move, and trees to speak.

Augurs and understood relations have

By maggot pies and choughs and rooks brought forth

The secret'st man of blood.

(III.iv.)

By the time Macbeth says these lines, Banquo has been murdered at Macbeth's command. Macbeth has been haunted by Banquo's ghost at what was supposed to be a celebratory dinner. The full horror of what he has done in order to achieve his ambition is now clear to Macbeth, and he warns his wife that the dead will have their revenge.

She should have died hereafter.

There would have been time for such a word.

Tomorrow, and tomorrow, and tomorrow

Creeps in this petty pace from day to day

To the last syllable of recorded time.

And all our yesterdays have lighted fools

The way to dusty death. Out, out, brief candle.

Life's but a walking shadow, a poor player

That struts and frets his hour upon the stage,

And then is heard no more. It is a tale

Told by an idiot, full of sound and fury,

Signifying nothing.

(V.v.)

After Macbeth learns of his wife's death, he utters these words. These lines form one of the most famous speeches in the play, revealing Macbeth's grief as well as his pessimism and despair. He says that life is pointless and meaningless, and that it's over too quickly. Macbeth's realization of the great evil he has done, which has brought about his wife's death, influences this speech as well. He is beginning to realize that the witches' second prediction will come true: Banquo's line will become kings, not his.

LADY MACBETH

O, never

Shall sun that morrow see!

Your face, my thane, is as a book where men

May read strange matters. To beguile the time,

Look like the time. Bear welcome in your eye,

Your hand, your tongue. Look like th' innocent flower,

But be the serpent under 't. He that's coming

Must be provide for: and you shall put

This night's great business into my dispatch,

Which shall to all our nights and days to come

Give solely sovereign sway and masterdom.

(I.v.)

In these lines, Lady Macbeth tells her husband to leave everything to her: She'll set up Duncan's murder that evening. In the meantime, she tells Macbeth, he should try to look as innocent as possible. The lines show Lady Macbeth pushing her husband to kill Duncan. We can't know if Macbeth would have decided to murder his king if his wife hadn't encouraged him so strongly.

> But screw your courage to the sticking-place,
>
> And we'll not fail. When Duncan is asleep—
>
> Whereto the rather shall his day's hard journey
>
> Soundly invite him—his two chamberlains
>
> Will I with wine and wassail so convince
>
> That memory, the warder of the brain,
>
> Shall be a fume, and the receipt of reason
>
> A limbeck only: when in swinish sleep
>
> Their drenchèd natures lied as in a death,
>
> What cannot you and I perform upon
>
> The unguarded Duncan? What not put upon
>
> His spongy officers, who shall bear the guilt
>
> Of our great quell?
>
> (I.vii.)

Lady Macbeth dismisses her husband's decision to let Duncan live and promises him that if he can act with courage, their plan can't fail. She tells Macbeth that once Duncan is asleep, she'll get his servants so drunk that they pass out. Then she and Macbeth can kill Duncan and blame his servants for the killing. Lady Macbeth's plan is good enough to convince Macbeth to change his mind and agree to kill Duncan.

> I laid their daggers ready;
>
> He could not miss 'em. Had he not resembled
>
> My father as he slept, I had done't.
>
> (II.ii.)

This short speech from Lady Macbeth reveals two important facts: first, that Lady Macbeth has not helped kill Duncan after all, and second, that Duncan's resemblance to her father prevented her from killing him. Lady Macbeth will have a complex reaction to the murder throughout the rest of the play, at times appearing to feel more genuine remorse than her husband for their actions. Her remorse will eventually lead to her suicide. These lines are an early suggestion that Lady Macbeth might not be as coldblooded as she claims to be.

> Out, damned spot; out, I say. One, two,
> —why, then 'tis time to do't.
> Hell is murky. Fie, my lord, fie, a soldier and afeard?
> What need we fear who knows it, when none
> can call our power to account?
> —Yet who would have thought the old man to
> have had so much blood in him.
> (V.i.)

Lady Macbeth sleepwalks through Macbeth's castle on the eve of his battle against Macduff and Malcolm. She is completely undone by guilt and has lost her mind. Similar to her husband's guilt-induced hallucinations, Lady Macbeth has started seeing things that aren't there—namely, blood on her hands, a physical manifestation of her guilt over her part in Duncan's murder.

BANQUO

> That, trusted home,
> Might yet enkindle you unto the crown,
> Besides the thane of Cawdor. But 'tis strange.
> And oftentimes, to win us to our harm,
> The instruments of darkness tell us truths,

Win us with honest trifles, to betray's

In deepest consequence.

(I.iii.)

Banquo muses on the events of the last few minutes: just as the witches predicted, Macbeth has been named thane of Cawdor. Banquo notes that just because the witches told the truth doesn't mean that they're not evil. Banquo understands far earlier than Macbeth that the witches don't necessarily have Macbeth's best interests in mind and their prophecies may turn out to be less positive than Macbeth believes.

Thou has it now: king, Cawdor, Glamis, all.

As the weird women promised, and I fear

Thou played'st most foully for 't. Yet it was said

It should not stand in thy posterity,

But that myself should be the root and father

Of many kings. If there come truth from them—

As upon thee, Macbeth, their speeches shine—

Why, by the verities on thee made good,

May they not be my oracles as well,

And set me up in hope? But hush, no more.

(III.i.)

Banquo's soliloquy reveals that he is suspicious of Macbeth, who, in becoming king, has achieved all that the witches promised for him. Banquo senses that Macbeth engaged in foul play in order to make the witches' prophecy come true. While the idea that Macbeth may have murdered Duncan fills Banquo with fear, the thought also gives Banquo hope that what the witches predicted for him will come true. He doesn't realize that in order for his sons to become king, he will have to die.

O treachery! Fly, good Fleance, fly, fly, fly!

Thou may'st revenge—O slave!

(III.iii.)

QUOTES AND ANALYSIS BY CHARACTER

These lines are Banquo's dying words, as he is slaughtered by the murderers Macbeth has hired. In his dying breaths, Banquo urges his son, Fleance, to flee to safety and charges him to someday revenge his father's death. This sets the stage for how the play will end, when Macbeth realizes that the Witches' prophecy will come true, and Banquo's children will rule Scotland.

MACDUFF

> *O horror, horror, horror!*
>
> *Tongue nor heart cannot conceive nor name thee!...*
>
> *Confusion now hath made his masterpiece.*
>
> *Most sacrilegious murder hath broke ope*
>
> *The Lord's anointed temple, and stole thence*
>
> *The life o' th' building!*
>
> *(II.iii.)*

Part of Macduff's work is to wake the king every morning. He discovers Duncan's murder and announces it to the rest of the people at Macbeth's castle. The heartbroken way he announces it spells trouble for Macbeth: Duncan was a beloved king. Macduff's lines of genuine horror and remorse at the death of the king contrast with the suspicion and distrust Macbeth's subjects will feel for him once he takes Duncan's place.

> *Bleed, bleed, poor country!*
>
> *Great tyranny, lay thou thy basis sure,*
>
> *For goodness dare not check thee.*
>
> *(IV.iii.)*

Macduff says these lines after having abandoned his wife and children and fled for his life. Beyond the danger Macbeth poses to Macduff personally, Macduff worries about what effect Macbeth's tyranny will have on Scotland. Here, Macduff is angry at himself and others who will not stand up to Macbeth. He will soon learn of

Macbeth's murder of his entire family and resolves to help lead the revolt against him.

> *Tyrant, show thy face!*
>
> *If thou beest slain, and with no stroke of mine,*
>
> *My wife and children's ghosts will haunt me still.*
>
> *I cannot strike at wretched kerns, whose arms*
>
> *Are hired to bear their staves. Either thou, Macbeth,*
>
> *Or else my sword with an unbattered edge*
>
> *I sheathe again undeeded. There thou shouldst be;*
>
> *By this great clatter, one of the greatest note*
>
> *Seems bruited. Let me find him, Fortune,*
>
> *And more I beg not.*
>
> *(V.vii.)*

Macduff is determined to kill Macbeth and revenge the brutal murder of his family, as this short speech makes clear. Macduff calls on Fortune to help him find Macbeth and kill him, echoing the role of fate and the supernatural in the play, as represented elsewhere by the witches.

> *Despair thy charm,*
>
> *And let the angel whom thou still hast served*
>
> *Tell thee, Macduff was from his mother's womb*
>
> *Untimely ripped.*
>
> *(V.viii.)*

Macbeth has already learned that Birnam Wood did move, as the witches predicted. Here, he learns from Macduff that the witches' last prediction has come true as well. As Macduff tells him, Macduff was taken from his mother's womb in a Caesarian section and thus was not "born." Macbeth is doomed.

NOTES

NOTES

11

WHAT DOES THE
ENDING MEAN?

AT THE END OF THE PLAY, Macbeth's severed head is brought to Malcolm by Macduff, proof that Macbeth has been overthrown and that Scotland is now Malcolm's to rule. Malcolm promises rewards to all who have fought for him and names them all earls, the first in Scotland. He announces that they will now work to welcome back all the people of Scotland who fled under Macbeth's tyranny and invites all present to watch him be crowned at Scone Castle, the traditional coronation site of Scottish kings. In his final speech, Malcolm also mentions that Lady Macbeth is said to have committed suicide. Thus, the play ends with very little ambiguity: the good side has won, and the evil side has been vanquished. Yet there is one remaining thread that is not resolved: that of Fleance, Banquo's son, who was able to flee his father's murderers. The witches predicted that Banquo would "get" kings, that is, be the patriarch in a line of rulers, although not becoming a ruler himself. Whether this will happen or not is unclear. Malcolm is the direct descendent of King Duncan (and, in historical fact, took the throne from Macbeth). There was a real Banquo, and King James I was thought to be descended from his line, so perhaps Shakespeare left the status of Banquo's descendants ambiguous in order to please his patron.

12

HOW TO WRITE LITERARY ANALYSIS

WHEN YOU READ FOR PLEASURE, your only goal is enjoyment. You might find yourself reading to get caught up in an exciting story, to learn about an interesting time or place, or just to pass the time. Maybe you're looking for inspiration, guidance, or a reflection of your own life. There are as many different, valid ways of reading a book as there are books in the world.

When you read a work of literature in an English class, however, you're being asked to read in a special way: you're being asked to perform *literary analysis*. To analyze something means to break it down into smaller parts and then examine how those parts work, both individually and together. Literary analysis involves examining all the parts of a novel, play, short story, or poem—elements such as character, setting, tone, and imagery—and thinking about how the author uses those elements to create certain effects.

A LITERARY ESSAY IS NOT A BOOK REVIEW

You're not being asked whether or not you liked a book or whether you'd recommend it to another reader. A literary essay also isn't like the kind of book report you wrote when you were younger, where your teacher wanted you to summarize the book's action. A high school– or college-level literary essay asks, "How does this piece of literature actually work?" "How does it do what it does?" and, "Why might the author have made the choices he or she did?"

The Seven Steps

No one is born knowing how to analyze literature; it's a skill you learn and a process you can master. As you gain more practice with this kind of thinking and writing, you'll be able to craft a method that works best for you. But until then, here are seven basic steps to writing a well-constructed literary essay:

1. Ask questions

2. Collect evidence

3. Construct a thesis

4. Develop and organize arguments

5. Write the introduction

6. Write the body paragraphs

7. Write the conclusion

1. ASK QUESTIONS

When you're assigned a literary essay in class, your teacher will often provide you with a list of writing prompts. Lucky you! Now all you have to do is choose one. Do yourself a favor and pick a topic that interests you. You'll have a much better (not to mention easier) time if you start off with something you enjoy thinking about. If you are asked to come up with a topic by yourself, though, you might start to feel a little panicked. Maybe you have too many ideas—or none at all. Don't worry. Take a deep breath and start by asking yourself these questions:

What struck you? Did a particular image, line, or scene linger in your mind for a long time? If it fascinated you, chances are you can draw on it to write a fascinating essay.

What confused you? Maybe you were surprised to
see a character act in a certain way, or maybe you didn't
understand why the book ended the way it did. Confusing
moments in a work of literature are like a loose thread in a
sweater: If you pull on it, you can unravel the entire thing.
Ask yourself why the author chose to write about that
character or scene the way he or she did and you might tap
into some important insights about the work as a whole.

Did you notice any patterns? Is there a phrase that the
main character uses constantly or an image that repeats
throughout the book? If you can figure out how that pattern
weaves through the work and what the significance of that
pattern is, you've almost got your entire essay mapped out.

Did you notice any contradictions or ironies? Great works
of literature are complex; great literary essays recognize and
explain those complexities. Maybe the title totally disagrees
with the book's subject matter. Maybe the main character
acts one way around his family and a completely different
way around his friends and associates. If you can find a way to
explain a work's contradictory elements, you've got the seeds
of a great essay.

At this point, you don't need to know exactly what you're
going to say about your topic; you just need a place to begin your
exploration. You can help direct your reading and brainstorming
by formulating your topic as a *question*, which you'll then try to
answer in your essay. The best questions invite critical debates
and discussions, not just a rehashing of the summary. Remember, you're looking for something you can *prove* or *argue* based on
evidence you find in the text. Finally, remember to keep the scope
of your question in mind. Is this a topic you can adequately address
within the word or page limit you've been given? Conversely, is
this a topic big enough to fill the required length?

Good Questions

*"Are Romeo and Juliet's parents responsible for
the deaths of their children?"*

"Why doesn't Hamlet kill Claudius right away?"

"Is Lady Macbeth a villain or a victim?"

Bad Questions

"What happens to Nick Bottom in A Midsummer
Night's Dream*?"*

"What do the other characters in Julius Caesar *think
about Caesar?"*

"How does Iago remind me of my brother?"

2. COLLECT EVIDENCE

Once you know what question you want to answer, it's time to scour
the book for things that will help you answer it. Don't worry if you
don't know what you want to say yet—right now you're just col-
lecting ideas and material and letting it all percolate. Keep track
of passages, symbols, images, or scenes that deal with your topic.
Eventually, you'll start making connections between these examples, and your thesis will emerge.

Here's a brief summary of the various parts that compose each
and every work of literature. These are the elements that you will
analyze in your essay, and that you will offer as evidence to support your arguments.

ELEMENTS OF STORY

These are the *whats* of the work—what happens, where it happens, and to whom it happens.

Plot: All of the events and actions of the work.

Character: The people who act and are acted upon in a literary work. The main character of a work is known as the *protagonist*.

Conflict: The central tension in the work. In most cases, the protagonist wants something, while opposing forces (antagonists) hinder the protagonist's progress.

Setting: When and where the work takes place. Elements of setting include location, time period, time of day, weather, social atmosphere, and economic conditions.

Narrator: The person telling the story. The narrator may straightforwardly report what happens, convey the subjective opinions and perceptions of one or more characters, or provide commentary and opinion in his or her own voice.

Themes: The main idea or message of the work—usually an abstract idea about people, society, or life in general. A work may have many themes, which may be in conflict with one another.

NOTES

ELEMENTS OF STYLE

These are the *hows*—how the characters speak, how the story is constructed, and how language is used throughout the work.

Structure and organization: *How the parts of the work are assembled.* Some novels are narrated in a linear, chronological fashion, while others skip around in time. Some plays follow a traditional three- or five-act structure, while others are a series of loosely connected scenes. Some authors deliberately leave gaps in their works, leaving readers to puzzle out the missing information. A work's structure and organization can tell you a lot about the kind of message it wants to convey.

Point of view: *The perspective from which a story is told.* In *first-person point of view*, the narrator involves himself- or herself in the story. ("I went to the store"; "We watched in horror as the bird slammed into the window.") A first-person narrator is usually the protagonist of the work, but not always. In *third-person point of view*, the narrator does not participate in the story. A third-person narrator may closely follow a specific character, recounting that individual character's thoughts or experiences, or it may be what we call an *omniscient* narrator. Omniscient narrators see and know all: they can witness any event in any time or place and are privy to the inner thoughts and feelings of all characters. Remember that the narrator and the author are not the same thing!

Diction: *Word choice.* Whether a character uses dry, clinical language or flowery prose with lots of exclamation points can tell you a lot about his or her attitude and personality.

Syntax: *Word order and sentence construction.* Syntax
is a crucial part of establishing an author's narrative voice.
Shakespeare, for example, is known for writing in iambic
pentameter, intermingling prose and verse, and scrambling
the usual word order of a sentence.

Tone: *The mood or feeling of the text.* Diction and syntax
often contribute to the tone of a work. A novel written in
short, clipped sentences that use small, simple words might
feel brusque, cold, or matter-of-fact.

Imagery: *Language that appeals to the senses;* representing
things that can be seen, smelled, heard, tasted, or touched.

Figurative language: *Language that is not meant to be
interpreted literally.* The most common types of figurative
language are *metaphors* and *similes,* which compare two
unlike things in order to suggest a similarity between them
—for example, *"All the world's a stage,"* or *"I'll warrant him,
as gentle as a lamb."* (Metaphors say one thing is another
thing; similes claim that one thing is *like* another thing.)

3. CONSTRUCT A THESIS

When you've examined all the evidence you've collected and know how you want to answer the question, it's time to write your thesis statement. A *thesis* is a claim about a work of literature that needs to be supported by evidence and arguments. The thesis statement is the heart of the literary essay, and the bulk of your essay will be spent trying to prove this claim. A good thesis will be:

Arguable. *"Julius Caesar* describes the political turmoil in Rome after the murder of Julius Caesar" isn't a thesis— it's a fact.

Provable through textual evidence. *"Hamlet* is a confusing but ultimately very well-written play" is a weak thesis because it offers the writer's personal opinion about the book. Yes, it's arguable, but it's not a claim that can be proved or supported with examples taken from the play itself.

Surprising. *"*Viola changes a great deal in *Twelfth Night"* is a weak thesis because it's obvious. A really strong thesis will argue for a reading of the text that is not immediately apparent.

Specific. "The relationships in *A Midsummer Night's Dream* tell us a lot about the fickle nature of romance" is almost a good thesis statement, but it's still too vague. What does the writer mean by "a lot"? How do the relationships tell us about the fickle nature of romance?

GOOD THESIS STATEMENTS

Question: In *Romeo and Juliet*, which is more powerful in shaping the lovers' story: fate or foolishness?

Thesis: "Though Shakespeare defines Romeo and Juliet as 'star-crossed lovers' and images of stars and planets appear throughout the play, a closer examination of that celestial imagery reveals that the stars are merely witnesses to the characters' foolish activities and not the causes themselves."

Question: Does Hamlet's misogyny prove his madness?

Thesis: "Hamlet's misogynistic behavior toward Gertrude and Ophelia can be seen as evidence that he really is going mad, because these scenes have little to do with his quest for justice, and yet they seem to provoke his strongest feelings. We see little evidence in the play that either Gertrude or Ophelia is guilty of any wrongdoing, yet he treats them both with paranoia and cruelty, suggesting that Hamlet has lost the ability to accurately interpret other people's motivations."

Question: How does blood function as a symbol in Macbeth?

Thesis: "Once Macbeth and Lady Macbeth embark on their murderous journey, blood comes to symbolize their guilt, and they begin to feel that their crimes have stained them in a way that cannot be washed clean. Blood becomes a permanent stain on the consciences of both characters, and it plagues them throughout life."

4. DEVELOP AND ORGANIZE ARGUMENTS

The reasons and examples that support your thesis will form the middle paragraphs of your essay. Since you can't really write your thesis statement until you know how you'll structure your argument, you'll probably end up working on steps 3 and 4 at the same time.

There's no single method of argumentation that will work in every context. One essay prompt might ask you to compare and contrast two characters, while another asks you to trace an image through a given work of literature. These questions require different kinds of answers and therefore different kinds of arguments. Below, we'll discuss three common kinds of essay prompts and some strategies for constructing a solid, well-argued case.

TYPES OF LITERARY ESSAYS

Compare and contrast

Compare and contrast the characters of King Lear and Gloucester in King Lear.

Chances are you've written this kind of essay before. In an academic literary context, you'll organize your arguments the same way you would in any other class. You can either go *subject by subject* or *point by point*. In the former, you'll discuss one character first and then the second. In the latter, you'll choose several traits (attitude toward life, social status, images and metaphors associated with the character) and devote a paragraph to each. You may want to use a mix of these two approaches—for example, you may want to spend a paragraph apiece broadly sketching King Lear's and Gloucester's personalities before transitioning into a paragraph or two describing a few key points of comparison. This can be a highly effective strategy if you want to make a counterintuitive argument—that, despite seeming to be totally different, the two objects being compared are actually similar in a very important way (or vice versa). Remember that your essay should reveal something fresh or unexpected about the text, so think beyond the obvious parallels and differences.

Trace

Choose an image—for example, birds, knives, or eyes—
and trace that image throughout Macbeth.

Sounds pretty easy, right? All you need to do is read the play, under-
line every appearance of a knife in *Macbeth*, and then list them in
your essay in the order they appear, right? Well, not exactly. Your
teacher doesn't want a simple catalog of examples. He or she wants
to see you make *connections* between those examples—that's the
difference between summarizing and analyzing. In the *Macbeth*
example above, think about the different contexts in which knives
appear in the play and to what effect. In *Macbeth*, there are real
knives and imagined knives; knives that kill and knives that simply threaten. Categorize and classify your examples to give them
some order. Finally, always keep the overall effect in mind. After
you choose and analyze your examples, you should come to some
greater understanding about the work, as well as your chosen
image, symbol, or phrase's role in developing the major themes and
stylistic strategies of that work.

Debate

Does Iago in Othello *hate women?*

In this kind of essay, you're being asked to debate a moral, ethical,
or aesthetic issue regarding the work. You might be asked to judge
a character or group of characters (*Is Caesar responsible for his own
demise?*) or the work itself (*Is* Romeo and Juliet *a feminist play?*).
For this kind of essay, there are two important points to keep in
mind. First, don't simply base your arguments on your personal
feelings and reactions. Every literary essay expects you to read and
analyze the work, so search for evidence in the text. What does Iago
have to say about women in *Othello*? How does Iago treat women
in *Othello*? As in any debate, you also need to make sure that you
define all the necessary terms before you begin to argue your case.

What does it mean to hate a whole gender? What makes a play feminist? You should define your terms right up front, in the first paragraph after your introduction.

Second, remember that strong literary essays make contrary and surprising arguments. Try to think outside the box. In the *Othello* example above, it seems like the obvious answer would be yes, Iago hates women. But can you think of any arguments for the opposite side? Even if your final assertion is that the play depicts an angry, misogynistic man who distrusts women, acknowledging and responding to the counterargument will strengthen your overall case.

5. WRITE THE INTRODUCTION

Your introduction sets up the entire essay. It's where you present your topic and articulate the particular issues and questions you'll be addressing. It's also where you, as the writer, introduce yourself to your readers. A persuasive literary essay immediately establishes its writer as a knowledgeable, authoritative figure.

An introduction can vary in length depending on the overall length of the essay, but in a traditional five-paragraph essay it should be no longer than one paragraph. However long it is, your introduction needs to:

Provide any necessary context. Your introduction should situate the reader and let him or her know what to expect. What book are you discussing? Which characters? What topic will you be addressing?

Answer the "So what?" question. Why is this topic important, and why is your particular position on the topic noteworthy? Ideally, your introduction should pique the reader's interest by suggesting how your argument is surprising or otherwise counterintuitive. Literary essays make unexpected connections and reveal less-than-obvious truths.

Present your thesis. This usually happens at or very near the end of your introduction.

Indicate the shape of the essay to come. Your reader should finish reading your introduction with a good sense of the scope of your essay as well as the path you'll take toward proving your thesis. You don't need to spell out every step, but you do need to suggest the organizational pattern you'll be using.

Your introduction should not:

Be vague. Beware of the two killer words in literary analysis: *interesting* and *important*. Of course the work, question, or example is interesting and important—that's why you're writing about it!

Open with any grandiose assertions. Many student readers think that beginning their essays with a flamboyant statement such as "Since the dawn of time, writers have been fascinated with the topic of free will" makes them sound important and commanding. You know what? It actually sounds pretty amateurish.

Wildly praise the work. Another typical mistake student writers make is extolling the work or author. Your teacher doesn't need to be told that "Shakespeare is perhaps the greatest writer in the English language." You can mention a work's reputation in passing—by referring to *Romeo and Juliet* as "Shakespeare's enduring classic," for example— but don't make a point of bringing it up unless that reputation is key to your argument.

Go off-topic. Keep your introduction streamlined and to the point. Don't feel the need to throw in all kinds of bells and whistles in order to impress your reader—just get to the point as quickly as you can without skimping on any of the required steps.

6. WRITE THE BODY PARAGRAPHS

Once you've written your introduction, you'll take the arguments you developed in step 4 and turn them into your body paragraphs. The organization of this middle section of your essay will largely be determined by the argumentative strategy you use, but no matter how you arrange your thoughts, your body paragraphs need to do the following:

Begin with a strong topic sentence. Topic sentences are like signs on a highway: they tell the readers where they are and where they're going. A good topic sentence not only alerts readers to what issue will be discussed in the following paragraph but also gives them a sense of what argument will be made about that issue. "Jealousy plays an important role in *A Midsummer Night's Dream*" isn't a strong topic sentence because it doesn't tell us very much. "Jealousy plays out most obviously among the quartet of Athenian lovers, who find themselves in an increasingly tangled knot of misaligned desire" is a much stronger topic sentence— it not only tells us what the paragraph will discuss (jealousy) but how the paragraph will discuss the topic (by showing how jealousy creates a set of conditions that leads to the play's climactic action).

Fully and completely develop a single thought. Don't skip around in your paragraph or try to stuff in too much material. Body paragraphs are like bricks: each individual one needs to be strong and sturdy or else the entire structure will collapse. Make sure you have really proven your point before moving on to the next one.

Use transitions effectively. Good literary essay writers know that each paragraph must be clearly and strongly linked to the material around it. Think of each paragraph as a response to the one that precedes it. Use transition words and phrases such as *however, similarly, on the contrary, therefore,* and *furthermore* to indicate what kind of response you're making.

7. WRITE THE CONCLUSION

Just as you used the introduction to ground your readers in the topic before providing your thesis, you'll use the conclusion to quickly summarize the specifics learned thus far and then hint at the broader implications of your topic. A good conclusion will:

Do more than simply restate the thesis. If your thesis argued that *The Merchant of Venice* can be read as a study of religious differences, don't simply end your essay by saying, "And that is why *The Merchant of Venice* can be read as a study of religious differences." If you've constructed your arguments well, this kind of statement will just be redundant.

Synthesize the arguments, not summarize them. Similarly, don't repeat the details of your body paragraphs in your conclusion. The readers have already read your essay, and chances are it's not so long that they've forgotten all your points by now.

Revisit the "So what?" question. In your introduction, you made a case for why your topic and position were important. You should close your essay with the same sort of gesture. What do your readers know now that they didn't know before? How will that knowledge help them better appreciate or understand the work overall?

Move from the specific to the general. Your essay has most likely treated a very specific element of the work— a single character, a small set of images, or a particular passage. In your conclusion, try to show how this narrow discussion has wider implications for the work overall. If your essay on *The Tempest* focused on the character of Prospero, for example, you might want to include a bit in your conclusion about how he fits into the play's larger message about power, humanity, or the pursuit of knowledge.

Stay relevant. Your conclusion should suggest new directions of thought, but it shouldn't be treated as an opportunity to pad your essay with all the extra, interesting ideas you came up with during your brainstorming sessions but couldn't fit into the essay proper. Don't attempt to stuff in unrelated queries or too many abstract thoughts.

Avoid making overblown closing statements. A conclusion should open up your highly specific, focused discussion, but it should do so without drawing a sweeping lesson about life or human nature. Making such observations may be part of the point of reading, but it's almost always a mistake in essays, where these observations tend to sound overly dramatic or simply silly.

A+ ESSAY CHECKLIST

Congratulations! If you've followed all the steps we've outlined above, you should have a solid literary essay to show for all your efforts. What if you've got your sights set on an A+? To write the kind of superlative essay that will be rewarded with a perfect grade, keep the following rubric in mind. These are the qualities that teachers expect to see in a truly A+ essay. How does yours stack up?

- Demonstrates a thorough understanding of the book
- Presents an original, compelling argument
- Thoughtfully analyzes the text's formal elements
- Uses appropriate and insightful examples
- Structures ideas in a logical and progressive order
- Demonstrates a mastery of sentence construction, transitions, grammar, spelling, and word choice

Suggested Essay Topics

1. The fantastical and grotesque witches are among the most memorable figures in the play. How does Shakespeare characterize the witches? What is their thematic significance?

2. Compare and contrast Macbeth, Macduff, and Banquo. How are they alike? How are they different? Is it possible to argue that Macbeth is the play's villain and Macduff or Banquo its hero, or is the matter more complicated than that?

3. Discuss the role that blood plays in *Macbeth*, particularly immediately following Duncan's murder and late in the play. What does it symbolize for Macbeth and his wife?

4. Discuss Macbeth's visions and hallucinations. What role do they play in the development of his character?

5. Is *Macbeth* a moral play? Is justice served at the end of the play? Defend your answer.

6. Discuss Shakespeare's use of the technique of elision, in which certain key events take place offstage. Why do you think he uses this technique?

A+ STUDENT ESSAY

Equivocation is the practice of deliberately deceiving a listener without explicitly lying, either by using ambiguously misleading language or by withholding crucial information. What is the significance of equivocation in Macbeth?

Macbeth is a play about subterfuge and trickery. Macbeth, his wife, and the three weird sisters are linked in their mutual refusal to come right out and say things directly. Instead, they rely on implications, riddles, and ambiguity to evade the truth. Macbeth's ability to manipulate his language and his public image in order to hide his foul crimes makes him a very modern-seeming politician. However, his inability to see past the witches' equivocations—even as he utilizes the practice himself—ultimately leads to his downfall.

Sometimes, equivocations in *Macbeth* are meant kindly, as when Ross tries to spare Macduff's feelings by telling him that his wife and son are "well." Macduff initially takes this to mean that his family is alive and healthy, but Ross means that they are dead and in heaven. More often than not, though, such ambiguous statements lead to harm. The witches' deceptive prophecies are perhaps the most destructive instances of equivocation. They tell Macbeth that he can never be harmed by anyone "of woman born," but they neglect to tell him that Macduff was surgically removed from his mother's womb and therefore doesn't fall into that category. Similarly, they tell Macbeth that he can't be defeated until Birnam Wood comes to Dunsinane, but they don't alert him to the possibility that the opposing army might advance on his castle under cover of branches cut from Birnam trees.

Macbeth ignores several signs that might have alerted him to the witches' deceptive capabilities. Banquo warns Macbeth to be wary of their predictions, since evil creatures will sometimes win people's confidence with "honest trifles"

—small truths—only to betray them more deeply in the future. Indeed, the witches promise Macbeth fame and honor while withholding important information about the consequences that will follow. If Macbeth had been listening closely to the witches' language, he might have picked up on the their potential for trickery himself. The three weird sisters greet Banquo with a series of riddling titles, hailing him as "Lesser than Macbeth, and greater" and "Not so happy, yet much happier." The phrases sound like nonsense, but in reality both assertions in each statement are true. Banquo will have a lesser title than Macbeth, but is the greater (i.e., more moral) man. He will not be as fortunate as Macbeth in the short term, as he will soon be assassinated, but he will ultimately be much more fortunate because he won't be made to suffer the everlasting torments of hell. At no point do the witches lie to Macbeth—he simply hears what he wants to hear and ignores the rest.

It is ironic that Macbeth falls for the witches' equivocations because Macbeth and his wife are master equivocators themselves. Duncan laments that there's no method with which one may find "the mind's construction in the face," meaning that it is impossible to know what a person is truly thinking just from his or her outward appearance. Lady Macbeth mimics this language when she directs her husband to look like an "innocent flower" in order to hide the "serpent" that truly lurks in his heart. The Macbeths know how to use imagery and appearance to conceal the truth, and sometimes they even use those skills on themselves. Macbeth asks the stars to extinguish their light so that his "eye" cannot see what his "hand" does. Similarly, Lady Macbeth asks the night to grow as dark as the "smoke of hell" so that her knife cannot see itself slash its victim. The Macbeths know that their acts are wicked, so they try to hide the knowledge of their deeds from their own consciousness. In a sense, they wish to equivocate to themselves.

Just before Macduff kills him, Macbeth swears that he will never again believe those "juggling fiends" that manipulate words and speak "in a double sense." However, it's possible that the three weird sisters are not "fiends," or demons, at all, but rather agents of morality who bring Macbeth to justice by trapping him with his own tricks. The drunken porter, imagining himself the keeper of hell's gates, pretends to admit "an equivocator that could swear in both the scales against either scale, who committed treason enough for God's sake, yet could not equivocate to heaven." One can imagine Macbeth receiving a similar welcome from the true porter of hell's gates.

GLOSSARY OF LITERARY TERMS

Antagonist
The entity that acts to frustrate the goals of the protagonist. The antagonist is usually another character but may also be a non-human force.

Antihero / Antiheroine
A protagonist who is not admirable or who challenges notions of what should be considered admirable.

Character
A person, animal, or any other thing with a personality that appears in a narrative.

Climax
The moment of greatest intensity in a text or the major turning point in the plot.

Conflict
The central struggle that moves the plot forward. The conflict can be the protagonist's struggle against fate, nature, society, or another person.

First-person point of view
A literary style in which the narrator tells the story from his or her own point of view and refers to himself or herself as "I." The narrator may be an active participant in the story or just an observer.

Hero / heroine
The principal character in a literary work or narrative.

Imagery
Language that brings to mind sense-impressions, representing things that can be seen, smelled, heard, tasted, or touched.

Motif
A recurring idea, structure, contrast, or device that develops or informs the major themes of a work of literature.

Narrative
A story.

Narrator
The person (sometimes a character) who tells a story; the voice assumed by the writer. The narrator and the author of the work of literature are not the same person.

Plot
The arrangement of the events in a story, including the sequence in which they are told, the relative emphasis they are given, and the causal connections between events.

Point of View
The perspective that a narrative takes toward the events it describes.

Protagonist
The main character around whom the story revolves.

Setting
The location of a narrative in time and space. Setting creates mood or atmosphere.

Subplot
A secondary plot that is of less importance to the overall story but that may serve as a point of contrast or comparison to the main plot.

Symbol
An object, character, figure, or color that is used to represent an abstract idea or concept. Unlike an emblem, a symbol may have different meanings in different contexts.

Syntax
The way the words in a piece of writing are put together to form lines, phrases, or clauses; the basic structure of a piece of writing.

Theme
A fundamental and universal idea explored in a literary work.

STUDY GUIDE

Tone

The author's attitude toward the subject or characters of a story or poem or toward the reader.

Voice

An author's individual way of using language to reflect his or her own personality and attitudes. An author communicates voice through tone, diction, and syntax.

A Note on Plagiarism

Plagiarism—presenting someone else's work as your own—rears its ugly head in many forms. Many students know that copying text without citing it is unacceptable. But some don't realize that even if you're not quoting directly, but instead are paraphrasing or summarizing, it is plagiarism unless you cite the source.

HERE ARE THE MOST COMMON FORMS OF PLAGIARISM:

- Using an author's phrases, sentences, or paragraphs without citing the source

- Paraphrasing an author's ideas without citing the source

- Passing off another student's work as your own

HOW DO YOU STEER CLEAR OF PLAGIARISM?

- You should always acknowledge all words and ideas that aren't your own by using quotation marks around verbatim text or citations like footnotes and end-notes to note another writer's ideas.

- For more information on how to give credit when credit is due, ask your teacher for guidance or visit www.sparknotes.com.

NOTES

NOTES

NOTES